MULTICULTURAL MYTHS AND LEGENDS

17 Stories with Activities to
Build Cultural Awareness

◆

by Tara McCarthy

MULTICULTURAL MYTHS AND LEGENDS

17 Stories with Activities to
Build Cultural Awareness

◆

by Tara McCarthy

SCHOLASTIC
PROFESSIONAL BOOKS

NEW YORK ◆ TORONTO ◆ LONDON ◆ AUCKLAND ◆ SYDNEY

ACKNOWLEDGMENTS

"The Crane Wife" is a retelling of a story by the same title from *Folktales of Japan* edited by Keigo Seki (series edited by Richard Dorson; translation by Robert J. Adams). Copyright © 1963 by University of Chicago Press. Printed with permission.

"The Dancing Children" is a retelling of a story based on the "Origin of the Pleiades" from the *Journal of American Folk-Lore*, XIII, 281.

"Daughter of the Star" is a retelling of "The Princess from Heaven" from *Myths and Legends of the Congo* by Jan Knappert. Copyright © 1971 by Jan Knappert, published by Heinemann Educational Books. Printed with permission.

"Eldest Son and the Wrestling Match" is a retelling of a story from *North American Indian Legends* by Henry R. Schoolscraft, published by J.B. Lippincott & Co., 1856.

"How the Horse-Head Fiddle was Created" is excerpted from *Chinese Folk Tales* by Louise Kuo. Copyright © 1979 by Louise Kuo. Used by permission of Celestial Arts., P.O. Box 7327, Berkeley, CA 94707.

"The Origin of the Volcanoes" is a retelling based on information drawn from *Hawaiian Mythology* by Martha Beckwith. Copyright © 1970, 1971 by University of Hawaii Press. Printed with permission.

"Plumed Serpent" adapted from "Plumed Serpent in Tula" from *The Serpent and the Sun* by Calvin L. Roy. Used by permission of Farrar, Straus & Giroux, Inc.

"The Talking Bird" is adapted from "The Story of the Talking Bird" in *Flying Sails of My Bookhouse* edited by Olive Beaupre Miller and published by The Bookhouse for Children, Chicago. Copyright © 1920, 1928 by Olive Beaupre Miller.

While every effort has been made to secure permissions, we may have failed in a few cases to trace the copyright holder. We apologize for any apparent negligence.

Designed by Sue Boria

Cover design by Vincent Ceci

Cover illustration by Donna Perrone

Interior illustration by Joanna Roy

ISBN 0-590-49645-X

12 11 10 9 8 7 6 5 4 3 2 1   4 5/9 Printed in the U.S.A.

TABLE OF CONTENTS

MYTHS

◆◆◆◆◆◆◆

Myths are ancient stories that have their roots in the sacred beliefs,
or cosmology, of groups of people long ago. The stories take place
in a remote past, in a time before historical time, and the main characters
are deities, semi-deities, or humans with extraordinary powers.
Myths represent the ways in which all cultures, before the advent
of modern science, sought to explain the origin of the world and of
human beings' relationship to it.

LEGENDS

◆◆◆◆◆◆◆

Legends, too, are explanatory stories. Like myths, they have fantastic
elements in them. Legends, however, are set in historical times
and in places that seem recognizable, and the main characters are humans.
Legends may grow up around historical people and events or may
be wholly imaginary.

USING MYTHS
AND LEGENDS
IN YOUR CLASSROOM

myths and legends are two major categories falling under the heading *folktale*, the other main categories being trickster tales; fables; pourquoi, or "why," stories; and fairy tales. Folktales are stories that were originally transmitted orally. Once the stories are written down, they become folk literature.

For students and teachers in the upper elementary grades and in middle schools, myths and legends have a particular appeal:

◆ The stories are exciting. They are full of adventures, wondrous events, and heroes and heroines who are larger-than-life.

◆ Like all good literature for this age group, myths and legends have an intellectual content that naturally invites readers to think about and discuss symbols, values, and applications of a story to their lives today.

◆ Myths and legends can enhance reading comprehension and critical thinking. As students compare, contrast, and evaluate the stories, they develop their ability not only to enjoy this genre of literature, but also to articulate *why* they enjoy it.

◆ Exposure to myths and legends can help boost students' writing skills. The stories have stock characters, reiterated themes and settings, and a predictable aura of fantasy and "impossibility" that make them highly accesible models for student writing.

◆ Myths and legends serve as natural springboards into other areas of the curriculum, thus helping to build and enrich an integrated curriculum.

◆ By reading myths and legends, students build their general literacy. For example, from their reading here of Greek myths they begin to understand references like "a Promethean task," "a Procrustean situation," "strong as Hercules," and "a Pandora's box." From reading the "star" stories of the Nilotic Alur of Africa, of the Chinese, and of the Onondaga and Chippewa-Ojibwa of North America, students begin to "read" the night sky more closely. Origin myths about the seasons, volcanoes, and disease and medicine help students distinguish between myth and science.

BUILDING APPRECIATION OF CULTURAL DIVERSITY

The myths and legends of a group of people incorporate the group's deepest values and beliefs. As young readers enjoy the stories, these values and beliefs unfold to them. For example, in reading the Toltec myth of Plumed Serpent, students discover that the Toltec believed that humans are as attracted to war as they are to peace. In reading the Cherokee myth of the origin of disease and medicine, students discover the Cherokee belief that all living things are interdependent

and that humans thus have a reponsibility to the natural environment. In the Japanese legend "The Crane Wife," students find the belief that it is best not to question one's good luck. While students may agree or disagree with these messages, the stories themselves explicate the cultural settings in which the beliefs evolved, and thus help young readers develop a respect for and an understanding of those particular cultures.

At the same time, in reading a corpus of myths from different cultures, students will find many commonalities among different peoples' myths and legends. Ancient stories from places as far apart as Zaire, Greece, and the American Northwest teach the wisdom of obeying authority. In the Toltec myth mentioned above, and in a legend from Persia and a myth from Scandinavia, there is a common thread about the perils of leadership. The Cherokee theme of human connection to all the earth is echoed in stories from Hawaii and Ireland. By enjoying myths and legends together, your students will not only come to appreciate their own ethnic heritage, but will also find that they have much in common with all people.

BUILDING CULTURAL CONNECTIONS ACROSS THE CURRICULUM

You can use the myths and legends in this book to reinforce or introduce skills and cultural understandings in different curricular areas. Below are some general examples of strategies and projects. (*Follow-Up Activities and Curricular Links* in the prefatory material for each section of this book suggest more specific applications.)

◆ **GEOGRAPHY** When introducing a story, use a globe or world map to show the country from which the story comes. If your students are already studying that area, discuss features such as bodies of water, climate, and natural resources of the region. Ask students to read or review the story to find hints of this setting.

◆ **SOCIAL STUDIES** (1) Invite students to use art books and encyclopedias to find out about the ways of life of the culture centuries ago: what people wore, the work they did, the food they ate, and the kind of structures they built for housing and for worship or other public occasions. Suggest that

students use this visual information to make illustrations for the myth or legend in this book or for a myth or legend they write. (2) Suggest that students find and share pictures and descriptions of the story's region-of-origin as it is today and then identify what is "modern" about it and what facets of the past remain. For example, in researching modern Mexico City, students will discover that ancient pyramid temples, such as the one Plumed Serpent lived in, lie just outside the bustling urban area. (3) Invite students who have recently come from other lands to retell legends or myths from their home culture. Ask the class to listen for similarities and differences among these stories and the ones in this book.

◆ **SCIENCE**   The stories in *Section 1: Origins*, as well as many of the stories in the other three sections, give fantasy explanations of how certain phenomena happen or were created. Invite students to find the scientific explanations or hypotheses for these phenomena. For example, after reading the Hawaiian myth, students can research and report on the formation of volcanoes; after reading about Thor and his hammer, students can find out what actually causes thunder; after reading the myth of Demeter and Persephone, students can draw or make models that show how earth's seasons result from the earth's tilt and its rotation around the sun.

◆ **THE ARTS**   Introduce your students to the music and visual arts of the cultural groups represented in the stories. (1) Reproductions of paintings and crafts from different cultures are available in many art books. Make copies to display in the classroom while students are reading and exploring a story. Discuss the forms and techniques and encourage students to try them out. Some students may be able to bring to class reproductions or authentic

examples of the objects, such as pottery or wall hangings. (2) You may wish to play taped music from the represented culture just before or after the class reads or listens to a story. (See page 127 in the Bibliography for sources.) Invite students to try to identify the kinds of instruments used (such as strings, wind instruments, percussion instruments, or voice), to duplicate the rhythms with classroom band instruments, or to act out the story with the music as a background.

HOW THE MYTHS AND LEGENDS IN THIS BOOK ARE ORGANIZED

Myths are not the same as legends (see page 7), yet both forms usually have two important functions that operate concurrently within the story:

1. *To explain how things came to be* ◆ In this sense, the ancient stories respond to questions like the ones very small children ask today: "What are the stars?" "Why is there winter?" "Where does fire come from?" and so forth.

2. *To justify a culture's rules, rites, and social system* ◆ Myths and legends may explain how rulers got their authority, why children should obey their parents, how people are to behave toward other living things, or what happens to those who defy custom and law.

This book groups myths and legends in categories that allow students to focus on these two functions recursively. The stories in *Sections 1* and *3* emphasize the first function, how things came to be. The stories in *Sections 2* and *4* focus on the second function, the justification of a culture's rubrics about human behavior. However, as your students move through the sections and discuss them, they will come to see how most legends and myths serve both purposes.

GENERAL TEACHING TIPS

1. Review the pages that introduce each section to help you plan your instructional strategy. The pages include:

◆ a synopsis and some background information about each story in the section; you may wish to share the background information with students before they begin to read.

◆ a suggestion for introducing the section to your students;

◆ suggested discussion questions for using with the whole class or with smaller groups; the first discussion question for each story asks for factual recall; the other questions encourage students to analyze or evaluate some facet of the story and to give their personal responses to the literature.

◆ follow-up activities, including cooperative learning suggestions, that tie in to other areas of your curriculum;

◆ a reading-and-thinking activity sheet that students can use before, during, or after their reading of the section stories.

2. Distribute copies of the stories and the activity sheets to students or pairs of students. Discuss with students the reading strategy or strategies you wish them to use.

3. Remind students to use the Pronounciation Guide on pages 123-124 to find pronunciations of proper names in the story. Encourage students to use the writing lines after each name to identify the person or place.

4. Provide follow-up myths and legends for students to read and discuss. Refer to the Bibliography on page 125 for suggested titles. Invite students to share the books with the class or with a discussion group by summarizing the myths or legends,

discussing the cultures from which the stories come, and comparing the stories with other myths and legends they have read.

A VARIETY OF READING STRATEGIES

You may wish to have the whole class get involved in a particular strategy for each story or section. Or, you may wish to form student groups and suggest that each group use a different strategy. Some of the strategies can be combined.

1. *Reading Aloud* ◆ This strategy is especially appropriate for myths and legends, because originally the stories were told aloud. The strategy also assures that poor readers or second-language learners get to enjoy the story fully. You or an adept student reader can read the story to the class or group, while other students follow along silently with their copies of the story. With longer stories, students can take turns reading aloud. After reading and listening, encourage students to ask questions they have about the story. Write questions on the chalkboard or on poster paper for use in discussion groups.

2. *Directed Reading* ◆ With directed reading, students are informed beforehand about what facts and ideas they are to especially look for in a story. This strategy is often helpful for students who experience difficulties getting at the "meat" of unfamiliar materials. To direct reading, write on the chalkboard the Questions for Discussion that appear in the section-opener pages.

Explain that students are to look for answers to these questions as they read the story. Students can then read the story independently or with a partner. For partner-reading, you may wish to team an adept reader with a classmate who is a second-language learner or who has special needs. The adept reader can help his or her partner identify material that helps answer the questions.

3. *Reading with a Peer Partner* ◆ Students whose reading ability is average or above average can team up to read a story together. This strategy allows students at the same reading level to read through the story at a convivial pace and to work together to solve any decoding or comprehension problems that arise. Partners can write questions about the story to use later in a discussion.

4. *Reading Independently* ◆ Students who wish to read a story on their own should also be encouraged to jot down questions they have about it. After reading, they can get together with another independent reader and share and compare their questions.

DISCUSSING THE STORIES

The main goal of discussing myths and legends is not to seek "right" answers, but rather to encourage students to understand general themes and to construct personal responses that show what these ancient stories mean to them. Discussions can begin with the questions in the section-opener pages. Point out how the questions that ask for opinions and personal ideas lead to lively discussions that help all students appreciate and understand the story better. Then invite students to pose some of the questions they have jotted down while reading or listening to the story. Encourage students to choose questions that call not for recall of simple facts, but rather for their classmates' personal reactions to and interpretations of the story. Continually provide students with plenty of models of questions like these, such as "Why do you think the Crane Wife had to leave when her husband found out who she really was?" "Why do you think Chih-nii is so eager to go back to the sky, even though she must leave her children behind?" "If Theseus were around today, what kinds of things might he do to make the countryside safe?" "If you went to Tir Na N-og, what things on earth

would you miss? Why?" "If you lived in Pwalo, would you like to have a star princess as your ruler? Explain why or why not."

After discussing a story, invite students to read aloud a section that they understand better as a result of talking about the story with classmates. Ask students to tell what more they would like to know now about the story characters or the culture from which the story comes.

FROM READING TO WRITING

Suggestions for retelling or dramatizing myths and legends are included in the Follow-Up Activities. In addition, many of your students will probably want to write myths and legends of their own, especially after they have discussed the stories in this book with you and their classmates. To this end, encourage students to keep individual Writing Folders to use as an ongoing source of story ideas. The folders can include

◆ copies of the myths and legends in this book;

◆ completed Activity Sheets;

◆ lists of story ideas that result from class discussion;

◆ results of or reports about Follow-Up Activities the student chose to do;

◆ lists of favorite characters and most exciting events in the stories;

◆ notes about other myths and legends the student has enjoyed.

Whether students write independently or with a partner, encourage them to use the writing process steps of brainstorming, drafting, conferencing, revising, and editing, and to illustrate their stories. Suggest that a good way of publishing a myth or legend is to read it aloud to classmates. If possible, tape record the tell-aloud stories so that students can listen to them again later. Students can also put their stories together in a classroom "Myths and Legends Anthology" to dip into and read and discuss with a partner. You may wish to make copies of the stories for a "Myths and Legends Magazine" to be presented to the library or that each student can bring home.

We think you'll find myths and legends to be exciting, thought-provoking, and useful additions to your classroom. Myths and legends are part of our common heritage. Once read, they are seldom forgotten: cognitively, they imbue students with a frame of literary reference that will serve them well as they study other genres; affectively, they reply to young people's needs to wonder, to imagine, and to discover what is valuable in their own lives.

ORIGINS

Because they seek to answer complex questions like "Why is there day and night?", "How did humankind harness the power of fire?"; "How did we establish the qualities a good leader must have?"; and "How did mischief and evil come to afflict human beings?", there is a sense in which all myths and legends are about origins. To introduce students to this pervasive element in ancient stories, this section offers two myths and two legends that deal with the origin of certain material, observable things or phenomena: the seasons, disease and medicine, musical instruments, and volcanoes.

SUMMARIES AND BACKGROUND INFORMATION

1. *The Origin of the Seasons: Demeter and Persephone* ◆ In this Greek myth, Demeter, the beneficent goddess of the earth's crops and soil, throws the world into year-round cold and famine when her beloved daughter Persephone is stolen from her by Hades, the god of the Underworld. Though Demeter succeeds in rescuing her daughter, there is a hitch: each year Persephone must return to Hades for seven months of the year. It's only for the five months that Persephone is returned to her mother that the earth becomes warm and fruitful again.

Demeter, worshipped for centuries in Greece, Asia Minor, and Sicily, was loved as a maternal figure for two reasons:

◆ Unlike the even-more-ancient goddess Gaea, who presided over earth in an abstract way, Demeter took care of humankind's practical concerns with soil, crops, and growing seasons. She was the personification of "Mother Earth."

◆ As the worship of Demeter grew over the centuries, her daughter Persephone entered the story. The fierce loyalty between the two women and their sorrow at being separated were recognizable as human emotions, in contrast to many other gods and goddesses and demi-deities who often seemed to have few affectionate feelings at all.

2. *The Origin of Disease and Medicine* ◆ In this Cherokee legend, animals seek ways to fight back against the humans who kill them. Afflicting humans with disease seems to be the only retribution. It is only the deer who decide that a human hunter will be spared disease if he or she offers thanks to the animal he or she killed. The kingdom of Plants, friendly to humans, provides remedies for many diseases inflicted by other endangered animals.

The Cherokee were farmers as well as hunters in their homeland, which originally covered about 40 thousand square miles in the Allegheny region of the United States. When white settlers and traders invaded this homeland, the Cherokee tried to establish co-existence by integrating into their ways of life some ways of the invaders: the raising of livestock and the building of schools, libraries, and mills. However, the newcomers wanted the Cherokee land itself. During the administration of President Andrew Jackson, most of the Cherokee were forced off their land and made to walk to Oklahoma to a "reservation." During this infamous journey, the "Trail of Tears," many hundreds of Cherokee died. Those who survived found themselves in an arid land where their old ways of sustenance, through fertile fields and verdant woods, were impossible. However, the legends—like this one—are still told.

3. *How the Horse-Head Fiddle Came To Be* ◆ In this legend from Mongolia, a young boy, Suho, lovingly raises a white pony. The pony, fleet of foot, is taken by the Khan, who subsequently kills the animal when it rears and throws him. The spirit of the pony returns to Suho and suggests a way for them to be together always: Suho is to use the bones, tendons, and hair of the pony to make an instrument that will provide music. Suho does this, and the horse-head fiddle, accompanied by song, becomes an integral part of the Mongolian culture.

The people to whom this legend belongs live in the Inner Mongolian region and in the Ch'inghai and Kansu provinces of China and were once ruled by a series of tyrannical Khans. The Mongolians' traditional lifeway was built around the herding and breeding of horses, cattle, and sheep. In their nomadic, often solitary existence, the herders came to relish their occasional meetings at oases, during which they sang to the accompaniment of horse-head fiddle music.

4. *The Origin of the Volcano* ◆ In this Hawaiian myth, Pele takes her younger sister Hi'iaku along with her as a companion as she seeks an island on which to build a home for their family. Because the family's spirits are made of fire, the home must be dug out of the earth where water cannot touch them and where the flames can escape through a cone. During her search for such a location, Pele meets and falls in love with a young man on the island of Kauai. Later, she sends Hi'iaku back to fetch him. The errand is delayed by dangerous adventures. Angry and jealous, Pele throws the young man into the volcano. Hi'iaku rescues him. According to the myth, Pele and her family inhabit volcanoes to this day.

The story of Pele exists in many forms throughout the South and North Pacific, where volcanoes are common and represent a destructive force and also a constructive one: the building-up of fertile land. In some renditions of the myth, Pele has many sisters who try to carry out her wishes. In other renditions, Hi'iaka is the main heroine and Pele a secondary one. On the islands of Hawaii, the myth of Pele not only accounts for the origin of volcanoes, but also for the origin of the *hula*, in which the many and varying episodes of the full story are told in dance, song, and gesture.

INTRODUCING THE SECTION

◆ Discuss myths and legends as ancient stories that people told long ago in an attempt to answer serious questions about how important things began. To focus on the "serious" and "important" aspects, students might review any lighthearted "Why" (Pourquoi) tales they've read, such as "Why Rabbit Has a Short Tail" or "How the Elephant Got Its Trunk" and then discuss how questions like the following deal with phenomena that are more important to human beings:

1. What accounts for the eruption of volcanoes?

2. Who invented musical instruments?

3. What are the causes of disease? How can we cure diseases?

4. How do farmers depend on regularly recurring seasons?

◆ Explain to students that most myths and legends not only seek to answer important questions, but also tell stories about human relationships. Although the characters in the stories are fanciful, make-believe, and magic in most ways, the problems they deal with are often the same kinds of problems real people deal with today.

READING STRATEGY: THINK AS YOU READ

You may wish to distribute Activity Sheet 1 (page 27) for students to use as they read and discuss the myths with a partner or a small group. Invite the class to preview the directions together. Students can share their responses after they read each myth or when they conclude the section. Suggest that they refer to their responses in the class follow-up discussion.

See page 14 for additional reading strategies you may wish students to use in this unit.

QUESTIONS FOR DISCUSSION

1. *The Origin of the Seasons*

◆ According to this myth, what was earth's climate like before Persephone was stolen away by Hades? Why did this climate change?

◆ In your opinion, was Demeter's revenge justified or unjustified? Why? What alternative actions might she have taken?

◆ In your opinion, what parts of the myth seem like make-believe? What are the parts that seem most realistic?

2. *The Origin of Disease and Medicine*

◆ In this legend, living things are divided into three groups: human beings, wild animals, and plants. How are the wild animals and plants in the story like human beings? How are they different?

◆ In your opinion, what are the lessons in this legend about the relationship of humans to the rest of nature?

◆ According to the legend, what are the sources of medicines that cure disease? From what you know about sources of some medicines, is this a realistic idea or a fanciful one? What does the legend tell you about Cherokee discoveries?

3. *The Origin of a Musical Instrument*

◆ What's the most realistic part of this legend? What's the most fanciful part?

◆ What does the legend tell you about the real-life ways of Mongolian people in days gone by? What does it tell you about their rulers long ago?

◆ Every group of people has some form of music and myths or legends that tell of its origin. Why do you think music is so important to human beings? What are some ways in which music is used?

4. *The Origin of the Volcano*

◆ Why do you think the people of the Pacific developed myths about the origin of volcanoes? What other land forms or natural phenomena would you expect to find explained in the myths of this region?

◆ In myths, gods and goddesses have supernatural powers but also often act like human beings. What are some of Pele's powers? How does she use them to act out her human feelings?

SUMMING UP

Invite students to read and complete the activity sheet on page 27. They can work independently to relate the ideas presented in myths to the problems real people face today.

FOLLOW-UP ACTIVITIES AND CURRICULAR LINKS

1. SCIENCE ◆ Invite the class to recall and brainstorm some of the "Why" questions they asked when they were little kids. Examples are: "Why is the sky blue?" "What makes clouds?" or "What makes goosebumps?" Write students' questions on the chalkboard. Ask partners to choose one of the questions and answer it in two ways: as a teller of legends or myths and as a scientist. They can use their imaginations to write the fantastic explanation; to answer as a scientist, they will have to do research to find the facts that explain the phenomenon, and then write a brief, factual report.

Suggest that both partners present their finished work orally to the class, one partner reading the myth or legend and the other reading the scientific report. Ask the audience to listen to find out what they like best in each answer.

2. DRAMA ◆ Cooperative groups can choose one of the myths or legends to dramatize for the class. Together, the group can reread the story to determine what scenes they will act out. In addition to deciding who will play the various roles, the group should choose a member to be the narrator and work together on what the narrator might say to begin the story and to link the scenes. In addition to actors and a narrator, the group can appoint a director, members to be in charge of making or finding simple props, one or two sound engineers to provide sound effects and music, and an announcer to introduce the play and the participants.

Give groups the option of writing scripts for their play or of getting to know their characters and cues so well that they can improvise the dialogue and the actions. You may wish to sit in on each group's rehearsals to help them solve any problems they encounter and to offer suggestions about diction, volume, and movement.

Before the plays are presented, help the class develop some criteria about what makes a good audience. Explain that at the conclusion of each play, members of the audience should be able to talk about what they liked best in the play, why they liked that section, and what role or other stagecraft chore they would like to have (and why) if *they* were presenting the play.

3. SOCIAL STUDIES ◆ Invite students to research the cultures represented in the stories to find out more about the following:

- ◆ The climate in Greece and the crops farmers raise there

- ◆ The methods of farming and food-getting the Cherokee used in their original homeland

- ◆ The Cherokee "Trail of Tears"

- ◆ The way of life of Mongolian herders

- ◆ The early migrations and voyages of the people of Polynesia

- ◆ The Pacific and Indian Oceans' "rim of fire"

Students can share their discoveries with the class and discuss how what they've learned adds to their understanding and appreciation of the myth.

4. ECOLOGY ◆ Discuss how the Cherokee myth draws on what this group learned about the medicinal properties of certain plants. Invite students to research recent findings about rain forest plants and why many scientists are thus alarmed at the destruction of rain forests. Use the outcome of this investigation as an opportunity to discuss the basic wisdom about the world and about human beings that is incorporated in myths.

5. MUSIC ◆ Invite students to find out how fiddles and other stringed instruments are made and then to construct a simple stringed instrument of his or her own. After demonstrating the instrument and telling classmates how it was made, invite the musician to work with a partner or a small group to make up a myth or legend about the instrument's origin.

Then and Now

The characters in myths and legends often have problems like the ones people today have. Read the words that the characters at the left are saying. When you read a story that has the same idea or message in it, write the title of the story in the second column. Then, in the third column, write about one or two real-life situations you know of that are examples of the same idea or message. One example is given to get you started.

Idea or Message	Story Title	An Example from Today
Humans can learn to use natural resources in responsible ways.		Many people recycle paper so that it can be used again.
Jealousy among young people can lead to destructive actions.		
It's sad to lose something you love, but you can make something beautiful as a way of remembering.		
Most parents will do anything they can to protect their children.		

THE ORIGIN OF THE SEASONS

GREECE

PART ONE
The Goddess Demeter and Her Daughter

Of all the gods and goddesses of Olympus, perhaps none were so much loved by humans as was Demeter. She was the goddess of the soil and of crops, and she tended them with great care all through the year, because she was concerned about human beings and wanted them always to have enough to eat. And so sunny, warm centuries went by, with farmers planting and harvesting their crops all year round.

But there was someone Demeter loved more than she loved any human, and this was her daughter Persephone. Persephone was as cheerful and loving as her mother was, and the two women spent much time together. And while Demeter went about her duties caring for the land, Persephone played with her friends in the woods, fields, and meadows.

Now it happened that there was someone else who loved Persephone, and this was Hades, God of the Underworld. He ruled a cold, dark kingdom, filled with the sad souls who had once lived above on the warm earth. No light filtered through into the dreary caverns and caves of Hades' land, and the god himself was miserable there.

Nothing could make him happy, he decided, except to have a young and lively wife. Hades had seen Persephone many times as she played with her friends, and this was the woman he wanted as a bride.

There was only one who could answer Hades' demand, and that was Zeus, the king of all the gods and goddesses. Zeus listened to Hades' request, then with some reluctance granted it.

Hades harnessed his horses to a huge iron chariot and drove them up through the earth to the field where Persephone was resting. The god of the Underworld seized her and carried her below to his gloomy kingdom. There, Hades told her, she would live forever with him, to the end of time.

PART TWO
The Grief of Demeter and Persephone

It's not difficult to imagine Persephone's feelings. She was frightened and despairing. She refused to eat or drink, though Hades tried to tempt her with many delicacies. All day and all night she wept and cried out for her mother.

Demeter, too was frantic and sorrowful. She had no idea how her daughter had disappeared, but she could hear Persephone's cries.

Roaming and searching through all of the land, Demeter could hear that beloved voice in the trees, in the wind, and in the waves of the sea. Covered in a gray veil and cloak, the goddess traveled the earth searching for her child, asking everyone she met if they knew Persephone's fate. No one knew. No one could help.

And so the sad years passed, until Demeter finally met a spirit named Helios, who could see into the past. Helios told the goddess where Persephone was and how she had been carried there by Hades and how Zeus himself had given his permission for this awful deed.

Now Demeter's grief turned to rage. She went to Zeus and demanded that Persephone be returned to her. The god refused. He had promised Hades this bride, and he would not go back on his promise.

PART THREE
Demeter's Revenge

What was necessary to convince Zeus to reunite Demeter with her daughter? The goddess's plan was simple and terrible. She ceased caring for the soil and the plants on which humans depended. She made cold winds blow constantly, clouded the sun, made the rain stop falling. She sent blights and disease to wither the crops. Nothing grew. Famine was everywhere. Humans began to starve to death and to die of the cold.

Zeus could not avoid seeing the devastation that Demeter had caused, nor could he be deaf to the prayers of human beings. He summoned Demeter and begged her to resume her duties. Now it was her turn to refuse!

"I will not restore the earth to its bounty and beauty," she said, "until you restore my daughter to *me*!"

Zeus had no choice. He loved the earth and did not wish to see it destroyed. He called Hermes, his messenger, to him and directed him to descend to the underworld with this command to Hades:

"Persephone is yours no longer. Send her back to her mother."

Though Hades was angry at this command, he was bound to obey the king of the gods. But Hades was also a crafty being. As the overjoyed Persephone prepared to go back to her mother, the god said to her, "Come, now that you are happy again, break your long fast and share a meal with me before you leave." He handed the girl a pomegranate, cool and juicy. Persephone bit into it but had time only to swallow seven of the seeds before the chariot swept her back to the surface of earth.

Demeter and Persephone embraced, so happy at first that they could not speak, only laugh and weep with joy. Then Demeter said, "My dear daughter, I hope you ate nothing at all while you were in Hades' dark kingdom. Please tell me this is so."

"Why, nothing at all, mother," answered Persephone. "Except seven seeds from a pomegranate that Hades gave me."

All traces of happiness left Demeter's face. She began to weep and rage again. "That is the work of that deadly trickster! For there is a rule that is even above the command of Zeus. It is that whoever eats any food in the Underworld is bound to go back there and stay forever."

The mother and daughter sank again into despair. But Zeus took pity on them. He decreed that Persephone would have to return to the Underworld for seven months each year — one month for each seed she had swallowed. But during the other five months, she would come back to live with her mother.

And so it came about that for seven months Demeter goes about weeping and mourning for her daughter, and the earth turns cold and barren as the goddess neglects it. But when Persephone comes back to her, Demeter is happy again, and there are five months of warmth and sun and gentle rain. ◆

THE ORIGIN OF DISEASE AND MEDICINE

NORTH AMERICA
CHEROKEE

In the earliest days of the world, animals could talk, and they lived in harmony with human beings. But as the centuries went on, humans multiplied and spread over the land, destroying not only the homes of animals, but also the animals themselves. For humans invented spears and blow guns and knives and bows and arrows to kill animals for their flesh and hides and feathers; and they invented hooks with which to catch and kill fish.

The Bears especially became victims of the humans' bows and arrows. And so they held a council to find a way to protect themselves. They decided finally that they, too, would make bows and arrows. With these, the bears would go to war against humans. But this was easier said than done. The bears could fell a tree and make bows and arrows from the wood alright. There was even a bear who was willing to sacrifice himself so that bowstrings could be made from his entrails. But when it came to actually using the bow, the bears' long claws got in the way.

"We must cut off our claws so that we can use our new weapons", said one

bear. But their leader, the great White Bear, objected to this.

"Without our claws, we cannot dig for food or climb trees to escape our enemies," said White Bear. "Better that we should give up this bow-and-arrow idea and go on relying on our claws and teeth in our attempt to save ourselves from our human enemies."

The deer, too, held a council with their chief, Little Deer. They finally agreed that there was no way they could escape the killing power of humans. But they also agreed that any hunter who killed a deer must immediately ask the deer's pardon and say a prayer of thankfulness. For after all, it was the fallen deer who gave humans flesh for food, hides for clothing, and bones for tools.

Little Deer, who is swift as the wind and can never be killed, said, "When one of our Deer tribe is killed, I shall run to the place where she or he has fallen and ask her or his spirit, 'Has the hunter asked for pardon for this deed, and spoken his thanks?' If the answer is 'No,' I shall follow the hunter to his cabin and strike him with rheumatism, so that he shall become crippled."

So it is that we humans ask forgiveness of the deer we kill.

After this, every tribe of animals that walk or crawl, swim or fly met to discuss the cruelty with which humans treated them and to find ways ways to punish them. Snakes and fish would send such nightmares to humans that they would lose their appetites and sicken and die. Birds, whom humans caught and roasted on spits over a fire, invented other diseases with which to afflict humans. In the end, almost every animal, even the insects, had invented a special illness to punish the people who made their lives miserable.

If the animals had had their way, perhaps all humans on earth would be dead by now. But humans were saved by the Plants, who are friendly to humankind and did not wish to see them wiped off the earth. The Plants, too, held a council; and every kind of plant —trees, shrubs, grasses, moss, herbs, weeds, flowers —became a source of medicine. For each disease humans brought on themselves through their cruel and thoughtless acts toward animals, there was a plant that could cure the disease.

It has been up to humans, of course, to find the plant that will cure a specific disease. If we are not sure which medicinal plant to use or how to use it, then we must ask the spirit of the plant to tell us. ◆

How the Horse-Head Fiddle Came to Be

by Louise Kuo

MONGOLIA

How was the Mongolian fiddle, our most popular musical instrument, created? Why was it decorated with the head of a horse? This is a very sad story.

There was once an orphan boy named Suho who lived in the Chahar district. His grandmother brought him up, and he helped her with the meals and other household chores, besides taking the sheep to graze. They had a score of sheep, but that was all. When Suho came of age at seventeen, he was a lovable lad with a talent for singing. The neighboring herdsmen often gathered in the evening to hear his songs of the pastureland.

One night, Suho failed to return. His grandmother and all the neighbors became quite worried as it grew late. The night was pitch black when Suho finally appeared with a small thing cradled in his arms. It was a pure white newborn foal!

Seeing all the bewildered, anxious faces around him, Suho said, "I saw this little white thing alone and helpless on the roadside. There was no sign of the mare. I was so afraid the wolves would get him that I brought him with me."

Suho gave loving care to the colt, and as time went by, it grew strong and beautiful. Everyone who set eyes on it, loved it. But, of course, it was especially dear to Suho.

One night, Suho was awakened by persistent neighing. Getting up from his sleep, he rushed from the yurt. He could hear great confusion and bleating in the sheepfold. The white pony was defending the sheep from a large, gray wolf. Suho drove the wolf away and turned to the pony. It must have been fighting for a long time. He could see it was exhausted and dripping with sweat.

"Oh, you white pony! Such a good fellow! You have saved the sheep," he said as he tenderly patted the horse and wiped down the sweat. He spoke gently as though addressing his dearest human friend. From that time on the two were never separated, not even for a moment.

One spring the Khan announced that there would be a horse race and the winner would marry his daughter. The news spread over the pastureland, and Suho's friends urged him to join the race.

On the day of the event, many strong, good-looking young men, dressed in their best, came riding on their steeds of various colors. Suho had decided to compete and arrived with his snow-white pony. At a given signal, the horses were off, galloping with the speed of a whirlwind. But the white pony was the first to reach the winning post.

"Call the rider of the white pony here," the Khan ordered from the viewing stand. When he saw that the winner was only a simple herdsman, there was no mention of the marriage, and instead he said, "You will be given three big ingots of silver for your horse. You may go home."

"What! Does he really think I'd part with my dearest companion?" Suho thought to himself in anger. But he answered curtly, "I have won the hand of your daughter. I have not come to sell my pony."

"You rascal! How dare a poor herdsman talk to me like this! Seize him!"

Suho was beaten unconscious and lay there until the crowds dispersed and friends came to take him away. The beautiful white pony was led away in triumph by the Khan.

Suho was nursed back to health by his grandmother and, within a short time, recovered completely.

Some days later when Suho was resting, he heard knocking and called out, "Who's there?" Nobody answered but the knocking persisted, whereupon his grandmother went outside to see.

"Oh, it's your white pony!" she called out in surprise.

Suho dashed from the yurt. He was so happy to see his pony. But happiness turned to grief when he saw seven or eight arrows piercing the body of his dear pony. Gritting his teeth, Suho stifled his own cry of pain as he pulled out the arrows. Blood instantly streamed from the wounded pony who died the next day.

What had happened? Well, the Khan was overjoyed that he had acquired the splendid white pony and gave a banquet to celebrate and exhibit the fine animal to his family and the nobles. When he tried to mount, the pony reared and threw him to the ground. Then it galloped at full speed through the circle of guests.

"Catch it! If you can't catch it, kill it!" the infuriated Khan ordered.

A shower of arrows rained on the helpless pony. But it managed to return to die near its own master.

How sad and unhappy Suho was! He mourned the loss of his pony, day and night, and could not sleep or rest.

One night as he lay tossing, he seemed to see the white pony as though alive. It came right up to him and he fussed over it, caressing it tenderly.

"Can't you think of a way for me to be with you always, dear master?" the pony asked, and after a while it said, "Make a fiddle with my bones."

The following morning Suho carved a likeness of his beloved pony's head from its bones and used it for the upper part of the fiddle. He used its tendons for strings and the hairs from its flowing tail for the bowstrings.

Whenever Suho played on the horse-head fiddle, the memory of his dearest friend came back to him. His hatred for the Khan increased as he recalled the unfair treatment. These thoughts went into his music and echoed all the desires and emotions of the herdsmen. Every night after work, people flocked to hear him play. Listening, they would forget their weariness of the day. ◆

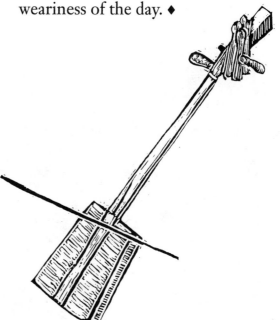

THE ORIGIN OF THE VOLCANO

HAWAII

PART ONE

The Fire Goddess Pele and Her Little Sister

Pele was one of six daughters and seven sons born to Haumea and her husband, Moemoe, on a distant, mystical island. Pele wished to build a new home for this large family of hers. She decided that a suitable house would be a huge pit, big enough to shelter them all in cool comfort when they were in their bodily forms. But in their spirit forms, the family was flame and clouds and lava, and so the house must have an opening at the top through which these fiery spirit forms could escape.

Pele determined that she would build this house somewhere on the beautiful islands that lay far away from her homeland. On her quest, she announced, she would take with her only her favorite little sister, Hi'iaka. Pele's brothers, Whirlwind, Tide, and Current, provided her with a canoe and paddles. Pele's family promised to follow her as soon as she had built a home for them. And thus the young goddess set off, holding her sister in her arms. From island to island went Pele and Hi'iaka. Awesome as each island was, none suited the goddess as a place for a home. For dig as she

might, as soon as Pele reached the ninth layer of earth, she could hear the roar of the sea beneath. And this would not do, for water is an unfriendly element to spirits made of flame.

In time, Pele and Hi'iaka reached the island of Kauai. And there something happened that would eventually change the loving relationship between Pele and her sister. For it was on Kauai, in the midst of a hula festival, that Pele met the young Kauai chief, Lohiau, and fell in love with him. As the sun rose and the festival ended, Pele promised Lohiau that the home she built would be big enough for him, too, and that she would send for him when her house-building was done.

On and on, from island to island, the two sisters traveled. At each place they stopped, Pele tried to dig a pit without hitting water. The goddess was finally successful on the island of Hawaii and settled there at the crater called Moku-a-weoweo (Land of Burning).

Now, announced Pele, it was time to send for Lohiau.

PART TWO
Hi'iaka's Journey

"It is you, Hi'iaka, who shall be my messenger," said Pele to her sister. "You must travel back to the island of Kauai and bring Lohiau here to Moku-a-weoweo."

Hi'iaka was reluctant. "How can I do that, sister?" she asked. "Such a journey is bound to be dangerous! I have no supernatural powers to overcome danger, as you do. And I am afraid to travel without companions. Besides, while I am gone, who will take care of the beautiful gardens I have planted here on Hawaii?"

"Well, then," said Pele, "I shall give you special powers for this journey to keep you safe. And you may take any companions you wish. As for your gardens, I will take good care of them while you are gone. But here are two warnings: first, you must return with Lohiau within forty days; second, you must not embrace him or show any affection toward him at all."

The sisters made this pact. And Hi'iaka chose for her companions her friend Thrush-Woman and her old nurse Skirt-of-Palms.

Even as they set off across the hills of Hawaii, Hi'iaka and her companions were beset with troubles. Evil monsters called mo'o—grinning and stunted— tried to capture them. Summoning up her new powers, Hi'iaka managed, just in time, to change the mo'o into strangely shaped rocks and tough, twisting vines, which can be seen to this very day on the island.

Then, after crossing the rough seas and coming ashore in Maui, the three travelers were pursued by a warlord, Chief Olepau. Three times the women had to disguise themselves in order to escape him. Once, they transformed themselves into an old woman, a child, and a dog; then, into three little girls stringing flowers to make necklaces; and finally, into three old women braiding mats for a new house.

These ruses worked, and the three women went on in their canoe to the island of Oahu. There they stopped for awhile, entranced by the misty, steep mountains, the abundance of fragrant flowers, and the singing sound of the wind and sea. It was this delay in their journey that caused the problem. For by the time they got to the island of Kauai, the young chief Lohiau was dead. He had died of grief waiting for the beautiful Pele he had met at the hula festival and despairing that she would ever send for him as she had promised.

Lohiau's family had buried his body in a cave at the summit of the highest cliff on the island. The cliff was as straight as a backbone and seemed impossible for one person to scale without help. Yet Hi'iaka, ever mindful of her promise to her sister Pele, struggled up to the tip of the stony slope. Reaching the cave, Hi'iaka chanted for ten days the special words that would bring Lohiau back to life. And indeed the chant brought Lohiau's spirit back into his body, and he was alive again. With Hi'iaka, Lohiau slid down a rainbow into the sea, and they began the long journey back to the island of Hawaii.

PART THREE
Pele's Revenge and Hi'iaka's Triumph

Far, far more than forty days had passed since Hi'iaka had left her sister Pele on Hawaii. Thrush-Woman and Skirt-of-Palms had gone ahead in their own canoe to tell Pele of the terrible trials and unforeseen adventures that had caused this delay.

But Pele was a jealous goddess and was convinced that her sister and Lohiau had fallen in love. So, even as her faithful sister and Lohiau skimmed over the ocean toward Hawaii, Pele set fire to Hi'iaka's beloved gardens. And she planned an even worse revenge.

As Hi'iaka approached the island, she could see the angry fire and molten rocks that flowed from the cone of Pele's home. Hi'iaka wept as she saw the flames consume the flowers she had planted and tended so carefully. Though saddened by all this, Hi'iaka went on to the shore with Lohiau. She could picture the joy with which Pele would greet them.

Pele met them, not with gratitude and happiness, but in a jealous fury. She threw Lohiau into the flaming core of the volcano and, along with him, Hi'iaka's companions, Thrush-Woman and Skirt-of-Palms. Finally, Pele encircled Hi'iaka with flames. But Hi'iaka still possessed the supernatural powers that Pele had given her and could not be destroyed by the volcano.

Now, for the second time, it was up to Hi'iaka to restore Lohiau to life. To do this, she must dig down through the layers of the volcano to find his body and restore his spirit.

On and on she dug, through layers of molten rock and swirling gusts of steam. Her fingers charred and shriveled in the fierce heat. On through the first level of the volcano, the second, the third. As Hi'iaka dug down into the fourth level, she found the bodies of her two women friends and restored them to life.

But Hi'iaka could not find Lohiau! Deeper and deeper she dug, until she reached the tenth level. Now, below her, she could hear the pounding of the sea, pounding with its vast waves as it tried to push upward through the volcano's cone and engulf the land. Hi'iaka knew that if she dug below this, the ocean waters would billow up through Pele's home and destroy the goddess of fire, destroy her very own sister.

Hi'iaka hestitated. In her loving kindness, she was torn between saving Lohiau and saving her sister. In this moment of hestitation, Lohiau's spirit was released. This spirit fluttered over the islands like a confused butterfly. Where should the spirit go? Where was the body to which it belonged? Two seabirds directed Lohiau's spirit to his body, which lay atop the Land of Burning.

The young chief, alive again, embraced Hi'iaka, the woman who had saved him. And it is said that Pele eventually accepted this union of her sister with Lohiau, so that all of them live together with the rest of Pele's family within the great volcano, to this very day. ◆

ORDER

DAUGHTER OF THE STAR

AFRICA • THE NILOTIC ALUR

••••••••

THESEUS AND THE MINOTAUR

GREECE

••••••••

PLUMED SERPENT

NORTH AMERICA • TOLTEC

••••••••

THE TALKING BIRD

PERSIA

••••••••

According to many scholars, myths and legends have practical functions within a culture. One of these functions is to to instill in people a respect for how order was established in their culture and for the rules and shared beliefs that maintain that order. The stories in this section point out (1) the rewards that ensue from following rules; (2) the hard task of bringing peace to a land; (3) the constant juxtaposition of peace and war; (4) the necessity of having intelligent, righteous people at the head of governments.

SUMMARIES AND BACKGROUND INFORMATION

1. *Daughter of the Star* ◆ In this myth told by the Nilotic Alur in Africa, a heavenly princess whose kingdom is a model of order falls in love with and marries a mortal king. When the king's subjects follow the princess's orders concerning the wedding feast, all goes smoothly. But when the princess returns to her sky kingdom to visit her parents, her husband's servants who accompany her disobey her instruction not to open a lidded jar. As a result, a swarm of locusts and other insects is released and attacks the servants. Unlike the similar story of Pandora (see Section 4), in this tale the pestilent insects are put back into the jar, and the servants thus learn to obey their rulers' instructions.

The Nilotic Alur live in Zaire near Lake Albert, just across from Uganda. Both these modern nations were once part of the great Kingdom of Kongo, which — before European invasions — stretched across much of Central Africa. The Alur's rites and ceremonies were built around their awareness of the need for rain. That is, good things came to them from the heavens if the people observed the rituals for bringing rain. The Daughter of the Stars is a personification of these "good things," and the rules she insists on reflect the regulations that the Alur's priests and wise men expected people to follow.

2. *Theseus and the Minotaur* ◆ There are many stories about Theseus, the mythic hero whom Greeks considered the ideal ruler because of his civilizing influence and insistence on "law and order." The myth here tells of his birth, of his journey to Athens to join his royal father, of how he slew monsters and established peace in the countryside, and finally of his encounter with the Minotaur on the island of Crete.

The Minotaur, a creature half human and half bull, lived in a labyrinth beneath the palace of King Minos, who demanded that Athenians send fourteen young men and women each year to satisfy the Minotaur's appetite. Theseus sails to Crete as one of the year's supposed victims. Ariadne, Minos's daughter, gives him a ball of twine, which he unwinds as he gropes through the dark labyrinth. He finds and slays the Minotaur, follows the twine back to the gateway, frees the other young Athenians, and sails home with them and Ariadne.

Archaeologists believe that the myth of the Minotaur may have grown up around a form of bullfighting or bullbaiting that was evidently practiced in ancient Crete. Paintings on artifacts show young men and women dressed in flowing costumes dancing around bulls and leaping over their horns.

3. *Plumed Serpent* ◆ In Aztec mythology, Quetzalcoatl, or The Plumed Serpent, and his people, the Toltec, brought civilization to Mexico. The story in this collection tells of how Plumed Serpent established peace in his kingdom through his own benign rule and through the simplicity, prayerfulness, and dedication to ceremony of his own daily life. Smoking Mirror, the god representing war, disorder, and bloodshed, is determined to establish his own rule in Tula, the majestic capital. He accomplishes this by showing Plumed Serpent his own image in a mirror. Aghast at how he has aged, Plumed Serpent begins to mourn his lost youth and forget his responsibilities to his people. To completely undermine Plumed Serpent, Smoking Mirror tempts him into a night of drunken revelry.

In the morning, saddened at what he has done, Plumed Serpent has his palace set afire and leaves his kingdom forever, so that it becomes the domain of the bloodthirsty Smoking Mirror.

The Toltec dominated the Mexican highlands from about A.D. 900 to 1200. Their chief city, Tula, or "Place of the Reeds"—now in ruins—contains several pyramids, one of which was Plumed Serpent's Temple. The Aztecs, who succeeded the Toltec, were greatly influenced by their language and culture, as were the Maya of Yucatán. Plumed Serpent fit into Aztec theology, which consisted of two religions, one dedicated to war and the other to peace and learning. This apparent contradiction was actually a recognition of the opposing forces in life and the double nature of human beings. The Aztecs believed that everything was created by this opposition.

4. *The Talking Bird* ◆ This Persian legend, a retelling of one in the *Arabian Nights*, tells of a gullible and foolish ruler, the Sultan Khos'roo Shah, who is tricked by his jealous sisters into abandoning his three infant children. The babies—two boys and a girl— are rescued and raised by a gatekeeper and his wife, who educate the children, give them every material advantage, and provide the love and guidance that enables them to grow up wise and brave; that is, having all the qualities a good ruler should have but which their royal father lacks.

The foster parents die, and young Princess Palizade and her brothers Bahman and Perviz are still unaware of their noble birth. A mysterious old woman tells them of a Talking Bird, a Singing Tree, and Golden Water. Determined to acquire these magical things, first Bahman and then Perviz set off to find them. Both young men are turned to stone when they forget to heed a dervish's warning about the dangers they will meet in their quest. Palizade, however, is successful: she brings her brothers back to life and the three carry the bird, the tree, and a flagon of the Golden Water back to their home. The Shah, journeying through the land, stops for a meal there. The Talking Bird tells him who the exemplary young people really are. The Shah repents of his past foolishness and names his children his rightful heirs.

The *Arabian Nights*, also called *The Thousand and One Nights*, were first collected in their written form in Arabic in the early 1500's and include such other familiar stories as those of Alladin, Sinbad, and Ali Baba. These stories come from Arabia, Egypt, India, and many other countries besides Persia. Persia, now Iran, has historically been a crossroads where civilizations met and blended. The story overarching all the tales is that of Scheherazade, who tells them to King Shahriyar over the course of 1,001 nights, always saving the end of a story until the next night, then beginning another. The King, who has heretofore killed his brides after one night with them, is so intrigued with the stories that he allows Scheherazade to live and, of course, eventually falls in love with her.

INTRODUCING THE SECTION

◆ Discuss how all groups of people, down through time and in all parts of the world, have leaders who construct rules for behavior. Explain that many myths and legends, like the four they are going to read now, tell why rules should be followed or describe the qualities an effective ruler or leader should have.

READING STRATEGY: THINK BEFORE YOU READ

You may wish to distribute Activity Sheet 2 (page 51) for students to use with a partner or small group as they share their own ideas about leadership qualities. Point out they should fill in the *Quality* sections in the idea web before they begin reading. As they read, they can write into each circle the name of a character who exemplifies that quality. The *Leader* section of some circles may remain blank. Students can add circles if they come upon mythic and legendary leaders who exhibit qualities that were not mentioned in the partner or group discussions.

See page 14 for additional reading strategies you may wish students to use in this unit.

QUESTIONS FOR DISCUSSION

1. *Daughter of the Star*

◆ According to this myth, what is the main difference between Niachero's and Mblukwa's kingdoms?

◆ Compare Niachero's kingdom with the kingdom of the Greek gods and goddesses. What is the main difference between the way deities behave in these two mythical kingdoms?

◆ How does Niachero impress upon the servants from earth the importance of following rules? In your opinion and from your own experiences with people, predict whether or not humans will continue to obey Niachero after she settles down permanently in their land.

2. *Theseus and the Minotaur*

◆ Why doesn't Theseus take the main road to Athens? What does his decision tell you about his character?

◆ Aegus doesn't want Theseus to go to Crete, but Theseus disobeys him. In your opinion, is Theseus's disobedience justified? Explain why or why not.

◆ Theseus is a super-hero. Yet at the end of the story, he makes a terrible error. What is this error? What does it show about even the bravest and most unusual super-heroes?

◆ How do you think life in Athens changes when Theseus returns home? To the Greeks, Theseus was known as the "civilizing hero." What do you think this term means? In what ways has Theseus civilized Athens and the lands around it?

3. *Plumed Serpent*

◆ How is Plumed Serpent different from most rulers of ancient times you've read about? How does his way of life help his people?

◆ In most myths, there are two opposing forces or characters who struggle for control. Who is the opposing character to Plumed Serpent? What does he represent?

◆ How does Plumed Serpent react when he sees himself in the mirror? In your opinion and from your own experience and knowledge, is this the usual way some people react to their old age? What kinds of things do you think Plumed Serpent wishes he had done as a youth?

◆ The Aztecs, who told this myth, believed that order and disorder follow one another through history. How does the ending of the myth of Plumed Serpent show this belief?

4. *The Talking Bird*

◆ In ancient Persia and in many other lands, rulers inherited their power and thrones from their parents. From what you know about the Sultan in this legend, what are some dangers in this custom? According to the same custom, the Sultan's children will eventually inherit his throne. In your opinion, will their rulership be different or the same as their father's? Why?

◆ Think about fairy tales you've read or heard. In what ways is this legend like a fairy tale? In what ways is it like the myth of Theseus and the Minotaur?

SUMMING UP

Invite students to compare and contrast the heroes and heroine of the three myths. How are their goals similar? (They all seek to establish order.) What is different about the ways they reach their goals?

Follow-up Activities and Curricular Links

1. WRITING *Transformations of Myths and Legends* ◆ Cooperative groups of four or five students can choose the legend or one of the myths in this section and write a transformation of it. This activity not only is fun and creative, but also provides students with new insights into the structure and theme of the story they've chosen to transform. Before forming groups, work with the whole class to brainstorm a chalkboard list of some ways a traditional story can be transformed. For example:

- ◆ Change or add details to the plot.
- ◆ Set the story in the modern world.
- ◆ Change a few of the main events.
- ◆ Change the point of view; for example, tell the story of Theseus from the point of view of the Minotaur.
- ◆ Change the gender of the hero or heroine.
- ◆ Write a sequel to the story.
- ◆ Write a story about what happened before the story in the book began.
- ◆ Keep the original story but add dialogue.

Students should also give their story transformations new titles.

After group members have decided what story they will transform and how they will do it, one member can act as scribe while the other students discuss and decide upon the plot steps. While two or three members use the scribe's list to write a rough draft of the story, other students in the group can draw illustrations for it and make a story cover. Groups should choose an editor and proofreader to go through the draft and indicate not only mechanical errors, but also places where details should be added or omitted. After the group has corrected the draft and made a clean copy, they can choose one member to read the transformed story to the class. Ask the audience to listen for the likenesses and differences between the original and the transformation. Has the basic message or theme of the original been retained in the transformation? What are the parallel events or characters between the old story and the new one?

2. MUSIC ◆ Read to the class the background notes on page 45 about The *Arabian Nights*. Then play a recording of Rimsky-Korsakov's symphonic suite *Scheherazade*. Explain that the music dramatizes some of the famous tales Scheherazade told. As each new tale begins musically, tell students its title. Some students may wish to find the written versions of these stories and read them silently as they listen to the music again. Suggest that students might also use the symphonic suite as background music as they read aloud or act out the legend of *The Talking Bird*.

3. SOCIAL STUDIES ◆ Invite students to find out about the different climates and topographies in central and southern Africa and draw a map to indicate them. Students can use their maps to predict the subjects and themes of myths in the different areas. For example, what kinds of mythical beings might figure in places where rivers are plentiful? in mountainous regions? in regions where rainfall is heavy? Some students may wish to follow up their predictions by finding and reading collections of African myths and legends.

4. MATH/ART ◆ The idea of a dark, winding, almost escape-proof maze of corridors, like the one Theseus encountered, is an intriguing one to most students. Invite students to work in small groups to construct models showing their interpretation of the labyrinth at Crete. Groups might want to make a pencil drawing of their maze first. As construction materials, they can use clay, papier-mâché, plasticine, or sheets of card-board held together with glue or masking tape. Groups can then make small clay or paper models of Theseus and the Minotaur and use them to act out the story.

To provide students with start-up ideas and some intriguing facts about mazes and labyrinths, you might have on hand one or more of the following books:

Anno's Math Games III by Mitsumasa Anno (Philomel, 1991). One section is on mazes and supplies many maze problems to solve.

Big Book of Mazes and Labyrinths by Walter Shepard (Dover, paper, 1973).

The Changing Maze by Zilpha Keatley Snyder and Charles Mikolaycak (Macmillan, 1985). This is a wonderful picture book for students of all ages. It emphasizes the mystical quality of mazes. A story is incorporated.

Groups can challenge classmates to find their way through the finished mazes, perhaps using a ball of twine to trace out possible paths.

5. ART ◆ Bring art books to class that show artifacts from ancient Greece. With students, read the descriptions of the pictures on vases, urns, and wall paintings, most of which show humans interacting with deities or semi-deities. Some students will enjoy illustrating the Greek myths they've read so far, using the painting style they see in the art book pictures.

Name(s) _____

What Makes a Good Leader

The stories you're going to read next tell about mythical and legendary leaders in different parts of the ancient world. Before you begin to read, think about and discuss the qualities you think a good leader should have. Then:

1. Write five of the leadership qualities you think are most important on the Quality lines in the five circles on the web.

2. If, as you read, you find a leader or leaders who have that quality, write his or her name on the Leader lines. In some cases, you may not find a leader who has a quality you've named.

3. As you read, you may come across a good leadership quality that you haven't noted on your web. If this happens, add circles to the web and fill them in.

QUALITY: _____

_____

LEADER: _____

QUALITY: _____

_____

LEADER: _____

A GOOD
LEADER

QUALITY: _____

_____

LEADER: _____

QUALITY: _____

_____

LEADER: _____

QUALITY: _____

_____

LEADER: _____

DAUGHTER OF THE STAR

AFRICA
THE NILOTIC ALUR

The Princess Niachero was called "Daughter of the Star" because her home was in the heavens, high above earth's highest mountain. Her kingdom was a peaceful, orderly place. For that very reason, Niachero was curious about Earth, where people seemed always to be breaking rules and bringing misfortune down upon themselves.

One day, as Niachero gazed down at the humans in a place called Pwalo, she saw Pwalo's young king, Mblukwa. Daughter of the Star immediately fell in love with him. She descended to Earth and announced, "I have come to marry Mblukwa."

Mblukwa happily agreed. What man would object to marrying a beautiful star-princess? "Let everything be made ready for the wedding!" the King commanded.

"And here are the rules you must follow for the ceremony," said Niachero to the people of Pwalo. "First of all, you must all bathe and scrub until you are spotlessly clean. Then you must put on fresh, clean garments. As for the wedding feast, you must not serve any black vegetables. Finally, with the porridge you may serve only meat."

"To hear you is to obey!" said the people. Everyone scurried about, washing themselves and their clothes. The women of the town prepared wonderful foods, following the star-princess's instructions.

The wedding feast lasted for three days, and was full of music and feasting and dancing. No one could remember a celebration that had gone so smoothly and happily.

Niachero stayed in Pwalo for a few weeks, and then said to her husband, "It is time for me to pay a visit to my family in the sky country. You must give me twenty-five goats to take to my parents as a gift."

Mbluka gathered the goats together and added two more as a special gift for his beloved bride. He also ordered six of his servants to accompany her on her journey. The people of Pwalo watched the long procession of goats and servants as the star-princess led them up from the village into the hills and to the base of the highest mountain. Still the people watched as the

princess urged her followers up the mountain, until they all looked like tiny dots. Then suddenly a huge cloud swooped down from the sky, enveloped the princess, the goats, and the servants, and carried them up to the heavens.

The sky-country echoed with the sounds of drumming and singing, in anticipation of the star-princess's return. Niachero took the six servants to a small, comfortable house. "Here you must stay until I come to fetch you for our return to Earth," she said. "Make use of anything you see here, except for those jars with lids on them. You may not open them at all."

Then Niachero ran off to see her family. They welcomed her with shouts of joy. "Our Daughter of the Star has come back to us!" said her father, hugging her. "And I am pleased with this fine gift of goats from your husband!"

"Come, join in the dance!" urged Niachero's mother.

Just as the sky-people were beginning to enjoy the Welcome Feast and the dancing, they suddenly stopped and looked up and pointed. A cloud of locusts was swirling above them, a whirring, buzzing swarm so thick and black it looked like a thundercloud.

"What is this?" they cried.

"These insects can come from only one place," said Niachero's father. "Is there anyone in the house-with-the-jars?"

"My servants from Earth are there!" said the sky-princess. She ran with all her family to the house-with-the-jars. Sure enough, the servants had disobeyed Niachero and had removed the lids of the jars. Now locusts were crawling all over them, until some of the servants seemed almost dead.

The sky-people quickly gathered the locusts from the sky and from the house itself, put them back into the jars, and put the lids back in place.

"Why do you Earth people do things like this?" said Niachero. "Now you see why I ordered you not to remove the lids from the jars. Why must you always do things that bring misfortune to you?"

Daughter of the Star went back to spend more time with her family. The servants, having learned their lesson, stayed in the house and left the jars lidded.

After a month, Niachero returned to the house and gathered the servants together. A cloud once again enfolded them. It carried them with their princess back to the base of the mountain. Daughter of the Star had returned to Earth to live with her beloved husband. ◆

THESEUS AND THE MINOTAUR

•••••••••••••••

GREECE

PART ONE
The Birth of a Hero

Aegeus, the king of Athens, often went traveling about over the land. Journeying one year far into the south, he met a woman called Aethra and fell in love with her. They were married, and soon Aethra bore an infant son, whom the couple named Theseus.

For a brief while, Aegeus took great joy in his wife and baby. But the responsibilities of kingship hung heavy on him, and he knew he must return to Athens and leave his family behind.

There were many tears at the parting. "Perhaps I shall never see you again," said Aegeus to Aethra. "But I hope one day to be reunited with my son. I shall leave my sandals and my sword here under the heaviest of rocks. If, when the boy grows up, he is strong enough to lift the rock, then he should take the sword and sandals and bring them to me in Athens. Then I shall know that the young man is Theseus indeed and that he is worthy to inherit my throne."

So saying, Aegeus left and went back to Athens, leaving Aethra to raise the boy alone. This she did with much dedication and love, and Theseus grew up to be a brave, strong fellow. In time, his mother knew he was ready to face the challenge of lifting the stone. Theseus did this easily and then put on his father's sandals and girded his father's sword around his waist.

"You know I must go now, Mother," he sad sadly to Aethra. "I must go to my father in Athens."

Fighting back her grief, Aethra agreed that it was so. She kissed Theseus goodbye, begging him to follow the main road so that he would meet as few troubles as possible on his long journey.

Now, Theseus was not one to disobey his mother. Yet the idea of a long journey with no adventures in it was not to his taste.

So instead of taking the main road to Athens, the young man instead traveled through the wild countryside. Each passerby he met warned him to turn back, for monsters of many kinds lay waiting in the forests and among the cliffs. "Then I shall slay them!" Theseus responded. "And the news of my deeds will precede me to Athens and make my father proud of me even before I arrive!"

The first monster Theseus encountered was Sciron, a robber who after taking all his victims owned, threw them off a cliff into the sea, where they were devoured by a giant turtle. Theseus slew Sciron and delivered him to the same fate. Soon after, the monster Sinis loomed into view. This creature had captured all who passed by. He tied them between the trunks of bent pine trees and then sprang the trees back so that the victim was torn to bits. But Sinis was no match for Theseus, who killed this monster, too, through his own ghastly method.

Many other monsters met their doom at Theseus's hand, and the people of the countryside felt freer now to enjoy their land. But one terrible creature remained, and his name was Procrustes. To each weary traveler he met, Procrustes offered a kind invitation to eat and rest in his home. Once the unsuspecting traveler was in Procrustes' den, the monster chained him to an iron bed, which fit no ordinary human at all. If the traveler was too tall for the bed, Procrustes would cut off his legs or his head to make him fit. And if the traveler was too short for the bed, Procrustes would stretch the chained victim out until he was pulled apart.

Now, Theseus had been warned of this monster, and so when he met him was ready to do away with him. Once he was in Procrustes' den, Theseus wrapped his sinewy arms around the creature and squeezed the life out of him. Then Theseus went to Procrustes' treasure room, found his gold and silver, and distributed it among the country people.

Thus Theseus arrived in his father's palace already a famous young man, much beloved by the people whom he had freed from the fear of monsters and toward whom he had been so generous. As he watched his son walk proudly into the royal courtroom, and as he saw the sandals and sword he had left for the boy, King

Aegeus wept with delight. Here, indeed, was the young man worthy to succeed him on the throne.

PART TWO
Meeting the Minotaur

Theseus and his father spent happy months together, but when spring arrived, Aegeus fell into deep gloom, as did all the citizens of Athens.

"Tell me what is wrong, father," begged Theseus.

"Now is the time for the tribute," Aegeus said mournfully. "Each spring it is thus. You see, my son, some years ago Athens went to war with Crete, and King Minos of that land laid siege to our city so that all here nearly died of starvation. Minos finally agreed to lift the siege only if we struck a terrible bargain with him." The king paused, scarcely able to go on.

"Continue, Father," said Theseus. "What is this terrible bargain?"

"Every year," said Aegeus, "we must send to Crete seven young men and seven young women. They sail away on a black-sailed ship, and they never return. For Minos puts them into a dark labyrinth deep beneath his castle, and there the young people are devoured by the Minotaur, a terrible beast that is half bull and half human."

"And do none of these poor victims ever find their way out of the labyrinth?" asked Theseus.

"None," answered Aegeus. "For the labyrinth was designed by the master architect Daedalus and has so many twists and turns in it that it is impossible to escape from it."

"This will happen no more!" said Theseus angrily. "This spring, I shall go as one of the seven young men, and I swear to you, father, that I shall meet the Minotaur and kill him!"

Now, Aegeus argued urgently against this. Having so recently found his son, he did not wish to lose him, especially to such a terrible fate. But Theseus would not be dissuaded. Girding on his father's sword, he prepared for the voyage to Crete.

The black-sailed ship stood ready in the harbor. The doomed young people walked tearfully aboard, as their families stood weeping on the shore. "Do not fear," Theseus said to his companions, "for I will save you." But they could not hear him, so grief-stricken and frightened they were.

Aegeus clasped Theseus to him and said, "Son, if by some chance you should succeed in this undertaking, remember to lower the black sail and raise a white one in its place. Then, looking out into the sea as the ship returns, I shall know you are still alive."

Theseus promised his father he would do so, and the ship sailed away over the horizon to the kingdom of Minos.

Now, Minos had a daughter named Ariadne. Unlike her cruel father, she deplored this terrible sacrifice of young lives each year. And this year, watching the heavy-hearted young Athenians come ashore, Ariadne saw one young man she knew she could not part with. This, of course, was Theseus, whose very appearance won Ariadne's heart immediately.

The fourteen victims were taken from the ship to a dank dungeon where they would spend one last night before being thrown into the labyrinth. After all was quiet in the castle, Ariadne crept down to this dungeon and found Theseus.

"Young man," she whispered. "I know of a way to escape from the labyrinth." She handed him a ball of twine. "Tomorrow, you must fasten one end of this to the gate of the labyrinth," she said. "Then unroll it

carefully as you proceed through the dark twists and turns. When the Minotaur charges you, swiftly follow the twine back to the gate. I shall be waiting there and will prevail upon my father to let you go home."

"Tomorrow is not soon enough," said Thesus, taking the ball of twine. "For I do not wish to escape the Minotaur, I wish to slay him and take all my companions home again. So, dear princess, will you show me the labyrinth now?"

Ariadne agreed to this. Stealthily she and Theseus crept from the dungeon and through the palace, where all lay sleeping, and came at last to the fatal gate. Theseus tied one end of the twine to it and bade Ariadne to wait for him there. Then, slowly unwinding the twine, he went down into the darkest maze he had ever imagined.

At first it was silent there, except for the sound of water dripping down the rocky sides of the labyrinth. Holding the unwinding twine in one hand, and groping with the other along the cold stones, Theseus made his way slowly along the tortuous twists and turns. He could see nothing, and he felt his heart beat faster as he

went farther and farther away from the gate. Silence still. Where was the beast? Theseus touched his father's sword, feeling some small comfort in it. On and on he went, until the ball of twine had grown very tiny indeed.

Suddenly Theseus came into an open court and heard a bellowing like thunder. This was the stable of the Minotaur, and the creature, taken by surprise, stood still for an instant. In that instant, Theseus could see the gigantic size and strength of his foe and feel the fiery, furious heat that emanated from its body.

The young man swifly drew his sword, meaning to stab the Minotaur in its heart as it charged him. But the

Minotaur was too wily to be killed so easily. Changing direction, it avoided the sword and charged Theseus from another direction.

Whirling and repositioning himself constantly to avoid the beast, Theseus was becoming exhausted. Though he had slain many other monsters before, none was as frightening as this one. And he could use only his sword hand to fend off the beast, for he had to keep hold of the twine with the other hand.

The Minotaur, almost as if it were playing with its victim, came closer and closer, until Theseus could feel its breath upon him and stare into its cruel eyes. Now the Minotaur was within sword's reach, and with a final thrust, Theseus plunged his sword into its heart. The creature fell to its knees, with a look of savage surprise, and then dropped to the ground, groaned, and toppled over.

Theseus backed away; then, sure that the Minotaur was dead, he turned and followed the twine back through the dark labyrinth until he reached the gate. There Ariadne awaited him. The two went silently back to the dungeon, bade the thirteen prisoners to be very quiet, then freed them from their cells. The dawn was just breaking as they ran to the ship and boarded it, and Ariadne, of course, went with them as they set sail for home.

There was great rejoicing and merriment aboard that ship as the grateful young people thanked Theseus and Ariadne for their deliverance. Theseus became totally involved in telling his companions about his struggle with the Minotaur. And so it was that he forgot his promise to his father.

Aegeus watched from a tower by the shore, straining his eyes to catch sight of the returning ship. Finally he saw it come over the morning horizon. But a black sail, not a white one, hung from the mast! So, believing his beloved son to be dead, the grieving king threw himself from the tower into the sea, which from ever after has been called the Aegean Sea, in his honor.

Theseus's adventure thus ended in sadness as well as triumph. ♦

PART ONE
Plumed Serpent and His People

In the time before Time, there was a young prince named Plumed Serpent, or Quetzalcoatl. Very early in his life, he showed special courage. When he was nine years old, his father, Cloud Serpent, was murdered. Plumed Serpent found the murderers and had them executed. Plumed Serpent was extraordinary in another way, too. He built a house for himself that was very plain and not princely at all. For four years he stayed in this house, praying and fasting and asking for forgiveness for any bad things he had done.

In the meantime, his people, the Toltecs, enjoyed a life of peace and plenty. They believed it was Plumed Serpent's wisdom and prayerful ways that brought them this long period of bounty, this long period without wars. Therefore, the Toltecs begged Plumed Serpent to be their king. With great reluctance, he agreed.

The people built a magnificent palace at Tula for their new king. It had seven huge pillars shaped like serpents. The walls were made of silver, gold, and pearl. Spanning the river, there was a bathing palace where

sparkling fountains glittered and blue streams flowed. In an underground treasure room, there were jewels, jade, and statuary made of precious gems and metals.

But Plumed Serpent did not use the glorious rooms of this palace. Instead, he kept one room as bare and dark as a cave, and that is where he stayed, praying and fasting and thinking for years on end. He had become a holy man as much as a king, and this life of solitude and plain living suited him best.

The Toltecs continued to flourish under Plumed Serpent's wise guidance. The corn grew so big that a farmer could carry only one ear of it at a time. Vines bore squash so huge that a grown man could not even get his arms around it. Cotton grew in every color of the rainbow.

From his plain, dark room, Plumed Serpent taught his people to love one another and to not shed blood. As peace prevailed over the decades, the Toltecs developed science and art. Studying the skies, they named the stars, predicted their movements, and developed calendars. Artisans learned to make objects of such beauty that they were unequalled anywhere else.

PART TWO
The Arrival of Smoking Mirror

Smoking Mirror, Tezcatlipoca, was the Warrior God. He was only content when humans shed one another's blood and when there was discontent and confusion over the Earth. And so Smoking Mirror was angry and jealous as he viewed the peaceful, orderly life of the Toltecs. He decided that he, not Plumed Serpent, must rule these people.

Among his many powers, Smoking Mirror was a magician who could change his shape and face in any way he wished. One day, disguised as a young man dressed in rich robes, he went to the door of Plumed Serpent's tiny room. He carried a mysterious package wrapped in cloth. When Plumed Serpent's guard stopped him and asked him to identify himself, Smoking Mirror said, "I can reveal myself only to the king, and I can show this gift only to him."

This answer intrigued Plumed Serpent, and he asked that the strange visitor be admitted.

"What have you come to show me?" asked Plumed Serpent.

"I am here to show you yourself," answered Smoking Mirror.

"There is nothing I need to know about myself," said Plumed Serpent. "I know what I am. I weep. I pray. I eat. I feel pain and joy. What else is there to know?"

Slowly Smoking Mirror unwrapped the package and brought out a mirror. He held it up to Plumed Serpent's face, and the king drew back in horror, then covered his eyes and began to weep.

"Is this what I have become?" he moaned. "I am an old man! My beard is long and knotted and gray. My limbs are shrunken. My skin is withered and spotted. What has happened to my youth?" In sorrow and fury, he dashed the mirror to the ground, breaking it. "I shall have a mask made for my face. No one shall ever see me this way again."

Smoking Mirror left the palace, satisfied and smiling cruelly. "Even a good king may be proud, or vain, or easy to hurt," he said to himself. "Now the way is clear for me to establish my power over the Toltecs."

And so Smoking Mirror began to wander about the land, creating havoc and hard feelings wherever he went.

He gathered crowds together by giving magic shows that caused riots and by beating strange music on drums that made people fight and destroy themselves and others. He set families and neighbors against one another. People who had lived together in peace for many years were now snarling enemies.

And what did Plumed Serpent do when he heard how his beloved kingdom was changing? He did nothing, for he was steeped in sadness that he had grown old. What had he done with his life? How much time was left to him? These were the only things he could think about.

Yet Smoking Mirror was not yet finished with bringing evil to Tula.

One day the Warrior God appeared at the door of the king's room, disguised this time as an old man. Plumed Serpent allowed him to enter.

"Look here," said Smoking Mirror. "I have heard that you, our king, are sad beyond all knowing. I have brought something to cheer you up, to make you feel young and energetic again." He held out a cup filled to the brim. "Drink this," said Smoking Mirror. "Your spirits will soar. You will be able to return to your priestly duties and be a good king again."

"But I am fasting today," said Plumed Serpent. "I have promised not to drink or eat."

"Just a sip," urged Smoking Mirror. He handed the cup to the king, who —weakened in will and spirit— drank all the liquid.

Immediately, he felt more cheerful and asked for another cup, then another. As Plumed Serpent drank, the magic wine made him forget his vows to live a simple life. He called for his nobles to come and join in a feast and celebration. Forgotten, too, in a mist of wine, were all the special ceremonies and prayers that the king was responsible for. Finally, late at night, Plumed Serpent fell into a wine-drugged sleep.

In the morning the king awoke, his heart heavy with shame for having broken his fast and for neglecting the ceremonies and prayers. He began to sob bitterly.

"I am no longer worthy to be king," he wept. "I shall have my palace burned, along with all its beautiful gardens, and I shall leave Tula to Smoking Mirror."

Plumed Serpent commanded his servants to set the many-colored birds in the garden free and then to set the palace ablaze. The King himself headed toward the rainlands and the country of boats.

At one point he stopped and took out a mirror and gazed straight into it. "Yes," he said to himself. "I am old. But I am no longer afraid of being old."

Some say that when Plumed Serpent came to the sea, he boarded a raft made of serpents and sailed to the Land of Wisdom. Others say that when he came to the sea, he set himself afire, and that his heart rose up from the ashes into the sky, where it became the morning star. ◆

THE TALKING BIRD

PERSIA

PART ONE
*The Foolish Shah
and His Children*

How overjoyed the Sultan Khos'roo Shah was when his wife the Sultaness told him that their first baby would soon arrive! But the Sultan's two sisters were jealous of the happy couple. When the little prince was born, they stole him away, placed him in a reed basket, and set the basket adrift on the canal.

When the Sultan came to see the baby, there was nothing in the cradle but a puppy! "Your wife has tricked you!" the jealous sisters said. "There was never any baby at all!" And the Sultan was foolish enough to believe this story.

Now, the baby prince was found by a gatekeeper who lived along the canal many miles from the Shah's palace. He brought the babe in its basket home to his wife. The couple was overjoyed to have a baby of their own. They named the child Bahman and showered him with love.

Twice again, the Sultaness announced that she was going to have a baby, and both times the Shah's sisters played their evil trick.

When another little boy was born, the sisters put a kitten in his cradle.

When a little girl was born, the sisters substituted a log of wood. Both times again, the foolish Sultan believed his sisters. Indeed he was so angry with the Sultaness that he condemned her to live in a small, iron-barred cell for the rest of her life.

The babies, like their older brother, had been set adrift in baskets. And, as before, the gatekeeper found the children and took them home to raise as his own. He and his wife named the second boy Perviz, and the girl they named Parizade.

No children had a happier life than did Bahman, Perviz, and Parizade. The gatekeeper and his wife worked hard to earn money and then built a beautiful home for their adopted children. The couple hired teachers to help the children excel at languages and fine manners and to learn riding and archery and footracing. The Princess Parizade often outdid her brothers in all their lessons, so that Bahman and Perviz developed a deep respect for her. There was scarcely a thing they would do without first asking her advice.

Life was cruelly interrupted for awhile when the gatekeeper and his wife died suddenly, within a few months of each another. They had never revealed to the children how they had been found. The princess and her brothers mourned for these good people for many months as the only mother and father they had ever known.

Fortunately, the old couple had saved a fortune that enabled Parizade, Bahman, and Perviz to live very comfortably in the beautiful home their adoptive parents had built for them.

PART TWO
The Quest

One day, when Bahman and Perviz were out hunting, an old woman came to the door and asked permission to enter and say her prayers, as it was the hour for doing so. Parizade welcomed her graciously and, when the woman had finished praying, invited her to have a meal of cakes and fruits.

As the old woman looked around her, she said, "This is indeed a beautiful home, filled with everything a person might desire. Yet there are three things missing."

"Oh, pray tell me what they are!" said Parizade.

"The first is the Talking Bird," said the woman. "It is such an amazing creature that when it speaks every bird in the land flies to gather around it. The second is the Singing Tree. Its leaves flutter in such a way that it makes a concert of sweet music. The third is the Golden Water. Just a single drop of it poured into a big vessel becomes a tall, bubbling fountain that never ceases to flow."

"And how might one find these three wondrous things?" asked Parizade.

"I hesitate to tell you," said the old woman. "For who knows what difficulties and dangers you might meet along the way? However, the road lies straight on from your home. You would travel along this road for twenty days. Then you would stop and ask the first person you saw. That person would tell you precisely how to find the Talking Bird, the Singing Tree, and the Golden Water."

With that, the old woman said goodbye to the princess and left.

When her brothers returned home, Parizade told them about the old woman and about the Talking Bird, the Singing Tree, and the Golden Water. Bahman determined that he would leave immediately to search for these treasures.

"Please don't do that," said his sister. "The woman warned of the many dangers that could beset you!"

"I'm not afraid," said Bahman. "But here, sister, I shall leave you this knife in its sheath. See how clean the knife is. Each day while I'm gone, pull the knife from its sheath. If ever you see blood upon the blade, you will know I'm in trouble and need your help. And now, there is not a moment to waste!" Bahman mounted his strong horse and went galloping away, the long road winding before him.

The twenty-day journey was an easy, pleasant one. At the end of the twentieth day, Bahman met an old dervish, or wise man, sitting in the road. "Pray tell me, my good fellow," said Bahman, "how I can find the Talking Bird, the Singing Tree, and the Golden Water."

"That is a dangerous quest," said the dervish. "Many people have undertaken it, and they have all perished. But if you insist on continuing, here is what you must do: ride your horse to the foot of the mountain over there in the distance, then alight and throw the bridle over the horse's neck. Proceed on foot to the top of the mountain. As you climb, you will see no one, but you

"Go back!" "What is the fool doing?" "Stop him! Catch him! Kill him!"

The voices rose into a din of menace and threat. Bahman's courage gave way. He turned to run back down the mountain, and immediately he was turned into a black stone.

At that very moment, many miles away, Princess Parizade pulled from its sheath the knife Bhaman had left her. It was covered with blood! In tears, she ran to her brother Perviz and showed him the bloody dagger. "Our brother is in danger, perhaps even dead!" she said.

"I will rescue him!" announced Perviz.

"No, let me do it," protested Parizade. "I am as strong as you and a better rider!"

"Usually I follow your advice, sister," said Perviz. "But this is a man's work. If you are afraid for me, take this string of pearls. Do you see how easily the pearls slide up and down the string? Each day, slide the pearls this way. If a day comes when the pearls will not move, you will know I am in trouble."

There was no stopping Perviz. Her heart filled with anguish, Parizade watched him ride off down the long road away from their home.

will hear many strange and confusing voices that will try to discourage you in every way. Pay them no heed. And be warned: never turn your head to look back. If you do, you will be turned into a black stone, like all the stones you will see around you. These stones were once adventurous people like yourself."

Bahman thanked the dervish courteously and went on his way. At the foot of the mountain, he reined in his horse, threw the bridle over its head, and began the long ascent on foot. Immediately he began to hear the voices the dervish had described.

It went with Peviz as it had with Bahman. An easy ride of twenty days, and then he met the dervish and listened to the old man's instructions. Like his brother, Perviz began to climb the mountian on foot. Like his brother, he heard the threatening voices and eventually was overcome with fear. Turning back, Perviz, too, was turned into a black stone. And at the very moment that that happened, Parizade found that she could no longer move the pearls along the string.

The Princess did not hesitate. Mounting her horse, she rode the twenty miles and met the dervish.

The dervish looked at her quizzically. "No woman has ever attempted this journey before," he said. "How will you thwart the voices that threaten you?"

"I shall put cotton in my ears so that I can't hear them," said Parizade.

"I admire your courage and your ingenuity," said the dervish. "If you do indeed reach the top of the mountain, you will find the Talking Bird. He will tell you how to find the Singing Tree and the Golden Water."

Stuffing her ears with cotton, Parizade climbed the mountain. The voices that threatened and struck others with fear she heard only as mumbles and gibberish. And so, unharmed, she reached the mountain peak, and there was the Talking Bird. He was a gorgeous, multi-colored creature with a voice like a violin.

"I am your servant forever!" the bird said. "Never before have I met anyone with such courage. I will consider it an honor to live in your home."

"Thank you, Talking Bird," said Parizade. "But I want not only you, but also the Golden Water and the Singing Tree."

"The Golden Water is just over there," said the Talking Bird. "Here is a tiny flagon for you to put some of it in. As for the Singing Tree, it is here beside me. But you need not uproot the whole thing. Just pluck off a branch. Plant the branch in your garden, and it will grow into another Singing Tree."

Parizade filled the flagon with Golden Water and took a branch from the Singing Tree. The Talking Bird hopped onto her shoulder. "Now we shall go with you to your home," he said.

"Not yet," said Parizade. "For I wish to find my brothers and bring them home with me."

"Easily done!" said the Talking Bird. "As we descend the mountain, scatter drops of the Golden Water on the black stones we pass by. Soon your brothers will be restored to you."

So on every black stone as she went down the mountain, Parizade threw a drop of the Golden Water, and the stones were transformed back into the hundreds of young adventurers who had failed at this quest. Parizade's beloved brothers were among this number. And thus, with the Talking Bird, the Singing Tree, the Golden Water, and the Princes Bahman and Perviz, Parizade returned to her home.

PART THREE
The Reunion

Parizade and her brothers spent many happy days rejoicing in being together again. In their garden, the Talking Bird sang his song and welcomed all the birds of the world, who were enticed by the melody. The Singing Tree added to the music with its fluttering concerts, and the Golden Water leapt and sang out in its fountain.

By and by, word came that the Sultan himself was making a tour of his kingdom and planned to stop for a

night at the home of Parizade, Bahman, and Perviz.

"Whatever shall we serve to an exalted being like the Sultan?" said Parizade.

"Cucumbers stuffed with pearls," said the Talking Bird.

"What a strange dish!" said Parizade. "Whoever could eat such a thing?"

"Trust me," answered the Talking Bird. So Parizade ordered the cooks to hollow-out the insides of cucumbers and stuff them with pearls.

The Sultan arrived with a procession of servants and horses and carriages full of baggage. As the ruler partook of the kind hospitality of Parizade's home, he remarked on the beauty of the Golden Water fountain, the music of the Singing Tree, and the vast number of birds fluttering about the Talking Bird's roost.

"Never have I seen a home so gracious and beautiful!" the Sultan exclaimed. But his happiness turned to alarm when he was served a dish of cucumbers stuffed with pearls!

"Who can eat such a foolish meal?" said the Sultan. "This is ridiculous!"

While Parizade and her brothers looked at one another in alarm at the

Sultan's displeasure, the Talking Bird spoke up. "Sultan," the bird asked, "is a cucumber stuffed with pearls any more ridiculous than three babies who turn out to be a puppy, a cat, and a log? Long ago, you believed that the Sultaness, your wife, passed off these things as your children. Was it not foolish of you to believe that?"

"But my sisters told me it was so!" sputtered the Shah.

"Your sisters were jealous women," said the Talking Bird. "And you should have been wise enough to know that. *These* are your children! These three exemplary young people are the children of you and the Sultaness. Your gatekeeper rescued them and raised them to be the courageous and fine people they are!"

The Sultan and his children stared at one another in wonder. Then there were many tears as they embraced.

Afterwards, the Sultan bowed his head in shame. "My poor Sultaness," he cried. "Through my own stupidity, I have made her a prisoner over all these many years! Come, my children, let us go to your mother. You will fill her heart with joy, and I will bow down to her in sorrow for the injury that I have done to all of you."

Thus the Sultan's family was reunited. The Sultanness, freed from her prison, rejoiced in her children. The Sultan resolved to be a wiser man, a fonder father, and a kinder ruler. Prince Bahman and Prince Perviz and Princess Parizade were welcomed with celebrations by all the people of the kingdom.

At Parizade's insistence, she and her brothers were allowed to live not in the Shah's palace, but rather in the home their parents who raised them had created for them. It was in this place that they had found love and that Parizade, especially, had found wisdom and knowledge, thanks to her own courage and to the Talking Bird. ♦

TRANSFORMATIONS

The myths and legends of almost all peoples take for granted a close interaction between human beings and other animals, plants, and non-living forms such as stars, rocks, mountains, and rivers. In myths, all life is sentient and wise, and humans and animals retain these qualities as they switch identities. Even the stars and other cosmic phenomena have human origins and ties. The stories in this section exemplify this theme of human connectedness with all the universe.

SUMMARIES AND BACKGROUND INFORMATION

1. *The Crane Wife* ◆ In this legend from Japan, a poor man rescues a crane from a fisher's net. Shortly thereafter, a beautiful woman appears at the man's door and convinces him to marry her. Whenever the man complans of his poverty, his wife relieves it by retiring to a small room and emerging many hours later with fabric so beautiful that her husband is able to sell it to the Emperor for a great price. Though the wife has made her husband promise not to intrude on her while she is spinning, the man's curiosity eventually leads him to open the door to the spinning room. There he sees the white crane he rescued. His promise broken, and her true identity discovered, the crane wife flies away and never returns.

In Japan, the crane is a symbol of long life and good luck. Today, Japanese children make strings of origami cranes to celebrate special occasions. The Japanese people also make millions of paper cranes as part of their demonstrations against nuclear weapons.

2. *Athena and Arachne* ◆ Among her many superhuman talents, the Greek goddess of wisdom, Athena, had some human ones, too, and one of them was weaving. In this myth, Athena challenges a skilled human weaver, Arachne, to a weaving contest. When Arachne's tapestry is judged to be the winner, Athena is enraged. In revenge, she turns Arachne into a new creature, a spider, and condemns her to spin until the end of time.

This myth is a potent example of how the ancient Greeks thought of their deities as having very human traits, including negative ones like envy, jealousy, and overweening pride. If your students have read the myth of Demeter and Persephone (Section 1, pages 28-30), you might ask them to recall the human traits the deities in that myth exhibit.

3. *The Dancing Children* ◆ This Onondaga myth tells of seven children who dismay their elders by dancing and frolicking all night on the shore of a lake where the group is camped for the winter. In spite of warnings from a mysterious wise man, the children continue their capers. Then, on one special night, the children ascend into the sky and become seven stars. In this form, they dance forever.

The Onondaga are a major tribe of the Iroquois Nation and lived in what is now Onondaga County in New York State. Onondaga myths show an unusal independence from outside influences. In general, Onondaga traditional stories were not affected by those of neighboring Native American nations, or by the stories brought by European settlers and explorers. Thus, the Onondaga story of the Dancing Children predates the incursion of Europeans on the North American continent. This is a fact you'll probably wish to share with students as they study the similarities between this myth and the Greek myth on pages 94-95.

4. *Chih-nii, the Heavenly Spinner* ◆ In this Chinese myth, Chih-nii, the daughter of a major deity, comes down to earth to bathe in a river. A simple cowherd, not knowing her identity, steals her robe and hides it, and—when the goddess comes to fetch it—convinces her to marry him. Unable to return to the heavens without her robe, Chih-nii consents to the proposal. Years later, Chih-nii cajoles her husband into giving the robe back to her. She returns to her kingdom in the sky. Through the good offices of a genie-ox, the cowherd rises into the sky and is reunited with his wife in the eastern sky. Her father appoints the cowherd to the guardainship of a star in the west. Each year the couple is reunited for a brief time by traveling a bridge over the Milky Way.

Chinese mythology reflects three different religions: Buddhism, Taoism, and Confucianism. Most of the divinities are Taoist in origin, but they often appear with other names as the three religions mixed and borrowed ancient tales from one another. An outstanding feature of Chinese mythology is that the pantheon of gods and goddesses reflects the earthly organization of Chinese government.

The sovereign god, the August Personage of Jade, demands regular accounts from the underling gods; he then elevates them or lowers them in rank or sometimes dismisses them entirely, according to how well they have carried out their duties. Functions remain, however: if a god is dismissed from the pantheon, another being, often a human, is appointed to take over the function. Sometimes new functions are created, too, as in the Chinese myth here, where the August Person of Jade's human son-in-law is appointed to be the god of a western star.

5. *Orion and the Sisters* ◆ Orion was a giant-sized hunter of prodigious strength. He was created by Zeus at the request of King Hyrieus of Boeotia, who had entertained Zeus most handsomely and who dearly wanted a son. Orion was such a passionate hunter that he offended even Artemis, the patroness of hunters, because he killed off all the wild animals of Crete. Orion then began to hunt young women, mainly the seven daughters of Atlas. Fleeing from the giant, the sisters prayed to Zeus for help. In response, Zeus turned them into doves; when they reached the sky, the doves became the star cluster called the Pleiades. Then Zeus, to keep Orion out of further mischief, also changed him, along with his dog Sirius, into a constellation.

The constellations of Orion and the Pleiades were used by the Greeks as seasonal forecasters. Orion and Sirius shine brilliantly in the winter sky, then fade as the winter wanes. The Pleiades begin to shine brightly in May, announcing the return of spring.

INTRODUCING THE SECTION

◆ Discuss fairy tales students have read or heard in which humans are magically transformed into animals. Examples are "The Frog Prince"; "Snow White and Rose Red," in which a prince is transformed into a bear; "The Seven Brothers," in which seven young princes are turned into swans and then regain their human shape with the help of their sister; and *Beauty and the Beast*, perhaps the tale most familiar to students because of the recent Disney movie.

Explain that two of the stories in this section tell about human-to-animal transformations, while the other three tell about another kind of transformation.

READING STRATEGY: THINK AFTER YOU READ

You may wish to distribute Activity Sheet 3 (page 82) for students to preview. Explain that they will be able to do the activity after they read all five stories. (Note: In doing the activity, students will begin to see similarities in the myths of different cultures.)

See page 14 for additional reading strategies you may wish students to use in this unit.

QUESTIONS FOR DISCUSSION

1. *The Crane Wife*

◆ Why does the Crane Wife leave her husband? Do think she was right to do so? Explain why you feel that way.

◆ In Japan, the crane is a symbol of good luck. What does this story have to say about how good luck comes to you? What does it have to say about how you lose good luck?

2. *Athena and Arachne*

◆ Athena is a powerful goddess. Yet she has some very human traits. What human traits does she show in this story?

◆ The ancient Greeks believed it was unwise for humans to compete with gods and goddesses. How does this story reflect that belief?

◆ Scientists refer to a certain class of animals as *arachnids*. What is one animal you'd expect to find in this group? Why? When you next see a spider, what will you think of?

3. *The Dancing Children*

◆ At the beginning of the story, how do the dancing children remind you of young people today?

◆ Do you think the ending of the story is happy or sad? Explain why you think so.

◆ What natural phenomenon does the story explain?

4. *The Heavenly Spinner*

◆ What are some of the reasons why Chih-nii stays on Earth so long? Why does she go back to the heavens?

◆ How does the August Personage of Jade behave toward the cowherd? Suppose this story were set in ancient Greece among the ancient gods and goddesses there. Do you think the cowherd's fate might have been different? Explain why or why not.

5. *Orion and the Sisters*

◆ Describe Orion's personality. What does he do that makes both deities and humans dislike him?

◆ How does Zeus help the seven sisters? In your opinion, is there another way he could have been more helpful? Describe it.

◆ What other story in this section does the story of the seven sisters remind you of? Tell about some of the likenesses and differences between the two stories.

SUMMING UP

Discuss the directions on Activity Sheet 3 (page 82). Suggest that students work with partners or in small groups to complete the activity, and then share and compare results with the class.

FOLLOW-UP ACTIVITIES AND CURRICULAR LINKS

1. MAKING CONSTELLATIONS ◆ Most students are fascinated by the mythic stories that explain and describe constellations. Students in your class can use sheets of black paper and star stickers or gold paint either to show the shapes of real constellations or to make up constellation shapes of their own. In either case, stories are part of the activity. Students will either find and retell traditional myths about real constellations or make up mythic stories to go with their original star patterns.

Because the glare of city lights at night makes it almost impossible for most of us today to see the constellations firsthand in their full glory, a trip to a planetarium or to a university observatory has become the next best way to experience the night sky as our ancestors did. If such a field trip is not practical or possible for you and your students, you might make available to them some of the many fine books that introduce children to the night sky. Suggestions:

Easy reading and good illustrations: *Stargazers* by Gail Gibbons (Holiday, 1992); *Sky All Around* by Anna Grossnickle Hines (Morrow, 1989)

For adept readers: *The Private Lives of the Stars* by Roy Gallant (Macmillan, 1986); *The Big Dipper and You* by E. C. Krupp (Morrow, 1989)

Students may wish to work on their constellations and write the accompanying stories independently or with a partner or small group. When it's time to share the stories, you can heighten the drama by turning down the classroom lights to simulate nighttime and have students sit in a circle while the storyteller tells the myth. When the story is ended, turn the lights back on and have the storyteller show the constellation. Conclude the project by displaying all the constellations around the room (or on the ceiling, if school policy permits this). Put the written stories in a folder on a reading table for students to reread and enjoy on their own.

2. STORY WEBS/STORY STARS ◆ Cooperative groups can choose one of the stories in this section and make a large, illustrated story web or story star to show the main events of the story. At the central point of the web or star, students can identify and show the transformation that takes place.

Discuss the activity with the class and organize the following materials in a central location:

◆ large sheets of tagboard from which to cut big circles or stars

◆ scissors, rulers, paste, paints and other art materials

◆ pencils, marking pens, notepaper, colored construction paper

Group members can work together to list in sequence the main events in the story they have chosen. Then the group can assign individuals or partners to write a sentence about one

Event: _____

Event: _____

TRANSFORMATION: CRANE TO WOMAN

Event: _____

Event: _____

Event: _____

of the events and illustrate it on a construction paper circle. Suggest that students write their sentences on scrap paper first. One or two group members can serve as editors to check the sentences for mechanics and spelling.

When the pictures and captions are done, the group can assign one or two members to draw and cut from tagboard a large circle (for a story web) or star shape (with one point for each story event). On circles, students can draw lines to replicate a spider web, with a heavy line leading outward to each story event. Group members can then paste their illustrations on the star points or web periphery to show the events clockwise, in the order in which they happened.

Groups can appoint a spokesperson to show their completed work to the class. Invite the audience to read the captions in order and add any details they recall from the story as they proceed to the next event. The class can display their story stars and webs around the classroom. Students may wish to invite younger children in your school to come to your room for a story hour and use the webs and stars as they tell the tales to their visitors.

3. ART/DRAMA ◆ Invite interested students to work independently or with partners to make stick puppets of main characters in one of the stories in this section. To encourage authenticity, bring to class several art books, encyclopedias, or other reference sources that show the kind of clothing worn by people of the culture represented in the myths. Encourage students to work these details into their puppets so that the puppets become "works of art" in and of themselves. Students may wish to get together to use their puppets in dramatizations of the stories in this section or of original plays in which characters from different stories meet and interact. You might keep the puppets in a central location for a while for students to use independently in other dramatizations.

4. SCIENCE ◆ Some students may be interested in researching a few of the more than 29,000 known kinds of spiders to find out how they are alike and how they are different. To present their findings, students can draw pictures or make models of kinds of spiders to show their actual size and coloration and use these visuals as they tell classmates about the animals. You might initiate the activity and guide the research by asking the class to brainstorm a list of questions they have about spiders. Encourage researchers to find the answers to the questions and to find other interesting and important data as well. Students can display their spiders on a table or bulletin board, with captions that identify them. You might use *Forms of Arachne* as a cumulative heading for the display.

TRANSFORMATIONS

Name(s) _____

Stars and Spinners

Fill in the charts to show how the stories in this section are alike and different.

STARS

Story Title	Who became the stars?	How did it happen?	Where does the story come from?

SPINNERS

Story Title	Who are the spinners?	What did they make?	Where does the story come from?

To Discuss: Stars and spinners appear in the legends and myths of people all over the world. Why do you think this is so? Jot down some of your ideas.

THE CRANE WIFE

•••••••••••

JAPAN

there was once an old man who earned a meager living by making charcoal, which his customers used in their stoves to make heat. It was not an easy life. The man always felt poor. Yet there was a kindliness in him that never waned, even when his pockets were empty.

The old man once saved enough money from his labors to buy a futon, or sleeping mattress. With much delight, he set out for the market. How wonderful it would be to have a mattress to sleep on, instead of the bare floor!

On his way to the market, the man met a fisher who had trapped a crane in a fishing net. The crane was struggling to get free, and the fisher was laughing at the poor bird's distress.

"Here! Let that bird free!" said the old man.

The fisher only laughed at him. "It's just a bird," he said. "Why worry?"

"Here!" said the old man. "Here is the money I have saved for a futon. I will give you this money if you will free the crane!"

"Done!" said the fisher. He took the money and freed the crane from the net. The bird immediately set flight on its wide, white, wonderful wings. The old man turned homeward, mourning the loss of his coins, but happily remembering the soaring crane.

Later that night, there was a soft knock at the man's door. He opened it and saw a beautiful young woman standing there.

"I wish to be your wife," the woman said.

The old man could scarcely believe his ears. "Why would you want to marry me?" he exclaimed. "I am old and poor."

"Nevertheless," said the woman, "it is you I want for a husband."

The old man protested just a little more, but he thought he knew luck when he saw it, and so he gladly consented to marry the woman. She became a tender wife and cared for him lovingly. The man's only wish was that he had more money, so that he could buy lovely clothes for his bride and provide her with a more comfortable home.

One night the old man sat by his charcoal stove, sighing over his poverty.

His wife said, "Perhaps I can help you, my dear husband. I am going to go into that tiny room there and close the door. I will be there for several hours. And you must promise me not to open the door to the room."

"Whatever you wish, my dear," sighed the man.

Many hours indeed! It was dawn before his wife reappeared. She was carrying a bolt of the most wonderful silky white cloth. "Here," she said, laying the bolt of cloth in her husband's arms. "Take this to the Emperor. He will give you a lot of money for it because there is no other cloth like it in the world."

The old man did as he was told. He returned with bags full of coins, enough to build a fine house, get a supply of good food, and buy clothes for his wife and himself. But then the money was gone.

"How shall I ever be able to maintain this house?" the old man sighed. "And when the food runs out and our clothes wear out, I have no way to replace them."

"Husband," said the woman, "you must excuse me again. I will go into the little room and close the door. By no means open the door while I am in there. You must promise me this."

"I promise," said the old man.

Once again the woman was gone for many hours. Once again she emerged from the room with a bolt of exquisite cloth. "Here," she said, giving the cloth to her husband. "The Emperor will want to buy this cloth, too, for it is even finer than the first bolt."

Indeed, the old man came back home with more bags of coins.

He said, "The Emperor is so pleased with the cloth you weave, my dear, that he has made us a promise. If I bring him another bolt of it, he will give us enough money to last us a lifetime."

"If that will please you, my dear," said the woman, " I will make some more of it." She walked toward the little room, saying, "But remember your promise: you are not to open the door."

The old man nodded in agreement. But as the night wore on, he was filled with curiosity about how his wife wove this extrordinary cloth. "Surely one little peek will not hurt," he said to himself.

He went to the door and opened it a crack. There was no woman there, but instead a beautiful white crane!

The crane turned her head and looked sorrowfully at the old man.

"Yes, it is I, who was once your wife," said the crane. "And the cloth I weave is from my own feathers. I have done this out of my gratitude to you

for saving me from the fisher's net. But now that you have discovered my secret, I can stay with you no longer."

And before the man could protest, the crane took flight through the window. The man rushed from the house and watched the crane wheel and swoop and finally disappear over the sea.

The man wept for the loss of his wife and for his own stupidity in breaking his promise to her. Sometimes he would walk down to the sea and look long at the cranes who nested on an island far out in the water. One crane was taller and more beautiful than all the others. She shimmered like the sun. "That is my crane-wife," the old man murmured. "She is the Queen of the Cranes." But she never came back to him. ♦

ATHENA AND ARACHNE

The goddesses and gods of Olympus had many powers at their command. What had they to fear from humans? What especially had Athena to fear? After all, she was the goddess of wisdom. Not only humans but also the other deities honored her for the sage advice she generously gave to whoever sought it.

Yet even Athena had a human side to her: she was immensely proud of her weaving. When she was not busy attending to the requests and pleas and questions of gods and humans, she sat at her loom making cloth and tapestries of unparalled beauty.

Now, down among the world of humans, there was also an expert weaver, and her name was Arachne. In the small village where she lived, she, too, sat at a loom and wove fabrics. Her neighbors and friends came each day to watch the shimmering pictures she worked into her cloth. Arachne's fame at weaving soon spread beyond the village, so that even the Nymphs, who were Athena's earthbound

servants, soon came to peek in the windows and watch Arachne at her work.

One day, as Arachne took from her loom an especially fine tapestry, her mother said, "Daughter, this is the best work you have ever done. Only Athena herself could do better!"

"Do *better*?" said Arachne indignantly. "Why, not even Athena could equal the cloth I weave!"

The Nymphs, listening outside the cottage, were astounded. How dare a mere human claim to be a better weaver than their mistress? The Nymphs hastened to Athena and told her of Arachne's boast.

Athena was indignant at first. But soon she was smiling calmly. "Let us teach this young woman a lesson," she said. "Arachne will soon learn that the works of a human can in no way equal the works of a goddess!"

Disguising herself as an old peasant woman, carrying her loom under her arm, and attended by her Nymphs, Athena paid a visit to Arachne's cottage one morning at dawn and knocked humbly at the door. When Arachne answered, Athena said, "The word of your weaving skill is known far and wide, young lady. Now, I am just an old woman, but I, too, have some skill at weaving. What do you say to a weaving contest? You and I shall set up our looms and make the finest cloth we can. Your family and friends and my attendants shall be the judges of the results."

Arachne happily agreed to the contest. She set up her loom next to the old woman's, and the weaving began.

As the sun rose high in the sky, marvelous scenes appeared on the looms. Each woman wove into her cloth the things she knew best. Athena wove pictures of the clouds and stars of her sky-kingdom and of the gods' and goddesses' view of Earth, with its winding rivers and snow-capped mountains. She wove thunderbolts into the cloth and visions of volcanoes and stormy seas. As the day wore on, the faces of all the gods and goddesses appeared in the fabric, and all who watched were in awe of this wonderful tapestry.

Arachne, weaving what she knew, made pictures of herders with their goats and horses, of mothers and fathers tending their children, of women bending over streams to gather water in their jugs, of families singing songs around soft, warm fires in the

having been before. How could a mere mortal outdo her? Throwing off her disguise, Athena showed herself as the great goddess she was, tall and glowing and fierce.

"So! It is weaving you like, Arachne, and weaving you are an expert at!" she stormed. "I shall make sure you weave until the end of the world!"

From the goddess's fingertips came sheets of light as she pointed toward Arachne. The girl began to shrink, and her face began to change. Quickly she was no larger than the bowl of a spoon, her body became round and many-legged, and her head was capped with tiny eyes that looked this way and that. Spinnerets of silk emerged from her small body. Arachne had become a spider, the very first one on Earth.

"With this silk you shall weave till time is done," said Athena.

And so it has been, with Arachne weaving exquisite webs down through all the centuries. And in the morning, drops of dew appear on the webs, which are Arachne's tears. ◆

evening, and of small boys and girls tucked into their beds at night. Arachne's family and friends nodded happily as these familiar scenes emerged on the cloth, and even the Nymphs, who'd never known exactly what human lives were like, were moved by them. And so, as the sun set and the time came to declare the winner of the contest, all those present declared that Arachne's cloth was the most beautiful.

At this decision, Athena was angrier than she could remember ever

THE DANCING CHILDREN

NORTH AMERICA
THE ONONDAGA

It was autumn, the time for the people to set out for a good hunting ground where they could set up camp for the winter. The chief, Hah-yah-no, knew where such a hunting ground lay. So families packed up a few belongings and followed their chief for several days through the countryside until they came to a beautiful lake surrounded by gray rocks and tall beech and chestnut trees.

The lake abounded with fish. Deer and bear came down to the lake to drink, squirrels ran and chattered among the trees, and rabbits bounded through the underbrush. This was indeed a good place to spend the winter!

Everyone set to work building lodges and gathering food. The children helped at all these tasks, but when everything was done, they grew bored. One night, seven of the children decided that they would have a dancing party by the shore of the lake. It was such fun dancing under the shimmering stars and by the light of the moon that the children decided that they would do this the next night, too.

But the next night, as the seven children danced and sang by the lake, a strange old man with shining white hair and dressed in white feathers appeared in their midst. The children stared at him. Who could he be? He was not one of their people.

"I have come to warn you," said the old man. "It is dangerous for you to come out alone here and dance in the night. Go back to your families and sleep."

The children paid no mind to him at all. They continued dancing that night as before, and as the weeks went by, their dances began earlier and lasted later. And each night the old man returned and repeated his warning.

There came a day when the children decided that they wanted to start their dancing even earlier. "We could do that," said one child, "if our parents would let us bring our evening meal down here to the shore of the lake."

But no parent would agree to this. "Children must eat at home with their families," the parents agreed. "That is the custom."

The children became rebellious. "If we can't have our meals by the lake," they decided, "then we shall not eat in the evening at all!"

So, hungry as they might be, the children whirled and danced and sang from sunset each evening far into the night. But one night a peculiar thing happened. As the children danced, they began to rise slowly into the air, until they were high above the lake and the lodges. Their parents saw them and ran with dishes of food, holding the dishes up and begging their children to return. But the children did not, or perhaps they could not. As their parents wept and pleaded with them, the young dancers ascended so high into the sky that they met the stars. And then they became stars, too.

The seven little starry dancers are still there in the sky. Whenever a shooting star races across the sky, their people are reminded of them and tell their story. ◆

CHIH-NII, THE HEAVENLY SPINNER

CHINA

C hih-nii was the daughter of the August Personage of Jade and therefore a deity herself. It was her duty to spin seamless clothes for her father and the rest of her family out of clouds and silk. It was a task Chih-nii enjoyed, yet she would sometimes grow weary of it and go down to Earth for awhile to enjoy the company of mortal young women. She especially enjoyed playing along the river banks with her human friends and swimming with them in the clear waters.

Now, near the river there lived a simple cowherd, He had a house, some land, and an ox to pull his plow. All he lacked was a wife, and he often complained that he would not be truly happy until he was married. The cowherd's ox was a genie in disguise, and hearing his master complain again one day about his need for a wife, the ox turned his head and said, "Master, go down to the river where the girls are swimming. Take one of the robes you find lying on the bank and bring it back here to your house and hide it. I guarantee you that you will get a wonderful wife in this way."

The cowherd did as he was told, taking from the river bank the first robe he saw. Rushing home, he hid the robe in a deep well in back of the house.

As it so happened, this was the robe of Chih-nii, and since she could not return to the heavens without it, she went in search of it. Knocking at the cowherd's door, she asked if he had taken her garment.

"I have your robe, but I shall never give it back to you," said the cowherd.

"But I insist!" said Chih-nii.

And so they argued back and forth; and as these things happen sometimes, they also fell in love and decided to marry.

The cowherd considered himself a thoroughly happy man. Soon he had not only his fine wife, but also two children to bounce on his knee.

Chih-nii said to him one day, "Now that we have been married so long and have children together, surely you can tell where you hid my robe on that long-ago day!"

The unsuspecting cowherd led his wife to the well and brought out her beautiful robe. When Chih-nii put it on, her entire countenance glowed with a starry lustre. Clearly she was a goddess, and the cowherd fell back in surprise.

"I must leave you, my husband," said Chih-nii. "For my home is in the heavens, not here on Earth." And saying that, she rose into the sky, leaving the cowherd and the children crying and begging her to come back.

Every day the babes wept for their mother, and the cowherd, too, was in despair. Finally the genie-ox took pity on them. "Master," he said, "put each of your children into a basket and tie the baskets to the ends of a long pole. Balance the pole on your shoulders. Then take hold of my tail and close your eyes. I will lead you to the heavens to rejoin your wife."

The cowherd did as the was told, and in the wink of an eye soon found himself standing before the throne of the August Personage of Jade, Chih-nii's father. He told the great god his sad story, and Chih-nii was summoned to say whether or not it was true.

How happy the goddess was to see her earthly husband and her two children! "Yes, father!" she said," all that the cowherd has spoken is truth."

"In that case," said the August Personage, " I shall make the cowherd a deity, too. And I shall give him a duty: he will be the god of a star over there to the West, across the River of Light, while my daughter stays here in the East with me."

Now, the River of Light is a vast and wide band of stars that crosses the night sky. When the cowherd and Chih-nii considered how immense the River of Light was, they feared they would be separated forever. "No, no, that is not so," the August Personage assured them." I will allow you to meet every seven days."

But the strange thing is that the cow-herd and Chih-nii misunderstood her father and thought he said that they could meet only once a year, on the seventh day of the seventh month.

And this is the pattern they have kept to over the centuries. On the seventh day of the seventh month, the couple eagerly prepares for the reunion. Because the cowherd and Chih-nii need a bridge to cross the River of Light, all the magpies in the world take twigs in their beaks on that day and fly to the River of Light to build a foot-bridge across it.

Some people say that it is always bound to rain in the morning of the seventh day of the seventh month. For the couple weep for joy as they embrace one another again, and their tears are so many and full that they fall to Earth. ◆

ORION AND THE SISTERS

GREECE

In the old days, the gods and goddesses sometimes went traveling about on Earth, visiting human beings. On one such occasion, Zeus, his messenger Hermes, and the ocean god Poseidon stayed for a while with King Hyrieus of Boeotia. The king entertained these important guests so lavishly that when it came time for them to leave, Zeus said to Hyrieus, "To reward your gracious hospitality, I will grant any one thing you wish."

"I have always wanted a son," answered the king. "A great big, strong son!"

"Easily done!" said Zeus. He threw a cowhide onto the ground. "Bury the hide, my friend," he said to Hyrieus. "In nine months it will emerge from the ground as the very son you wish for!"

Hyrieus did not question these directions. He did as Zeus told him, waited patiently, and was rewarded in due time when a son pushed his way to the surface. And the son emerged not as an infant, but as a full-grown man, and taller and stronger than any other human on earth. So tall was Orion that he could walk on the bottom of the sea without wetting his head. This was indeed much more than Hyrieus had asked for.

The son announced that his name was Orion and that he was leaving immediately to go hunting, for hunting was what he loved best to do. He strapped a huge bow and a quiver of arrows over his mighty shoulders. Then he whistled. "Here, Sirius!" he commanded. And as if by magic, a huge dog appeared at Orion's side and was never to leave it.

Orion proceeded to stride through the lands and isles of Greece, hunting and killing animals with abandon. On the island of Chios, Orion met the princess Merope. "I will impress her with my prowess as a hunter," thought Orion to himself, and he slew all the animals of the island. So horrified by this was Merope's father that he had a magician cast Orion into a deep sleep and remove him from Chios.

Orion awoke, having learned nothing at all from this experience. He proceeded to the island of Crete to continue his ravaging of the wildlife. But he had not figured on meeting a powerful goddess there. She was Artemis, the goddess of hunters, and though she also liked to use her bow and arrow to bring down a deer or a boar, she only did this when she needed food.

"Be warned, Orion!" she said to the giant hunter. "I will not tolerate your killing animals solely for sport!"

But Orion only laughed at her. Roaming the island, he soon had killed all the animals there, too.

Artemis's fury knew no bounds. "Look here, mighty hunter!" she said, and she pointed to a scorpion, knowing that this was the only animal Orion feared. "This scorpion shall pursue you to the ends of the Earth and deliver you its fatal sting if you ever shoot another animal!"

For a while, the frightened Orion put his bow and arrows down. But the desire to hunt was still strong in him, and he soon thought of a way to indulge it. "Artemis said I must not hunt wild animals," he thought, "but she said nothing about hunting *people*."

Returning to his homeland of Boeotia, Orion looked around for human quarries. It was not long before he saw seven lovely sisters running and playing in the hills. They were called the Pleiades, and they were the daughters of the god Atlas and a human mother named Pleione. So graceful and kindly were the Pleiades that they were admired and loved by all the deities as well as by every human they met. So it was a great shock to the sisters when they saw the giant Orion pursuing them and sending out deadly arrows in their direction.

As the thunderous footsteps of the hunter and the howling of his dog Sirius drew closer and closer, the sisters realized they could never escape on their own. Weeping with fear, they prayed to the god Zeus to rescue them. Zeus answered their prayer by transforming the sisters into seven beautiful white doves. In this form, the Pleiades flew high enough to escape Orion's arrows. And when the doves reached the top of the sky, they in turn became seven stars.

By this time, the deities were thoroughly angry with Orion for his incessant mischief and cruelty, so that Zeus transformed the hunter and his dog into stars, too, so that they could do no more damage on Earth. In the night sky, people ever after pointed to Orion and Sirius, who seem still to be pursuing the little cluster of Pleiades. Of course, Orion will never catch them. And to make sure that he must remember this, Artemis has turned the deadly Scorpion into stars and set the animal hot on the heels of Orion. ◆

WISDOM

THOR AND HIS HAMMER

SCANDINAVIA

········

THE STORY OF OISIN

IRELAND

········

PROMETHEUS AND PANDORA

GREECE

········

ELDEST SON AND
THE WRESTLING MATCH

NORTH AMERICA ◆ CHIPPEWA-OJIBWA

········

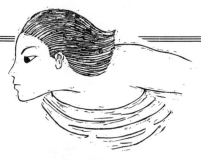

In myths and legends, as in all good stories, the characters learn something about themselves or about human nature in general. In these ancient stories, the message or lesson is so primal and "gutsy," so timelessly relevant, that it usually strikes a familiar chord even in modern readers and thus remains in their memory. What is learned goes beyond simple facts and falls into the realm of wisdom: knowledge and judgment based on experience. The wisdom in a particular tale can usually be stated as the theme of the tale.

Students can use the stories in this section to practice finding the themes, and thus the wisdom, in all the myths and legends they read.

SUMMARIES AND BACKGROUND INFORMATION

1. *Thor and His Hammer* ◆ In this myth from Scandinavia, Thor the Thunder god loses his hammer through his own carelessness. Helpless to defend Asgard, the home of the gods, without his hammer, Thor must find a way to get it back from the Frost King who has stolen it. The Frost King says he will return the hammer only if the goddess Freyja consents to marry him. Because Freyja refuses such a marriage, Thor disguises himself as the goddess and goes with the trickster god Loki to present himself as the bride. The Frost King is taken in by the ruse and gives the hammer to his "bride." Thor then throws off his disguise, slays some of the Frost Giants, and returns with his hammer to Asgard. One theme that can be found in this tale is that those in power must guard their power closely.

The male gods in Teutonic cosmology were usually involved in power struggles, warfare, and feats of physical daring as they jockeyed for political dominance. Freyja was one of a subset of deities called the Vanir. The Vanir were peaceful and benevolent and were guardians of harvests, pastures, fields, forests, sunlight, and rain.

2. *The Story of Oisin* ◆ In this Celtic myth, the king of the mystical land of Tir Na N-og is told that he will lose his power if his daughter marries, for then his son-in-law would become king. To destroy her chances of finding a husband, the king changes the hapless girl's head into the head of a pig. Advised by a Druid that she will regain her beauty if she can get a human named Oisin to marry her,

the princess goes to Eire (Ireland), finds Oisin, and so moves him with her sad story that he consents to wed her.

He goes to Tir Na N-og with the princess — now restored to her original beauty — and becomes ruler of that happy land where no one ever grows old. In time, Oisin yearns to see his homeland and his family again, even though his wife tells him that three hundred years have passed since he was there. Oisin, warned to never let his foot touch the earth, travels back to Eire on his wife's white horse. Leaning from the saddle to see his father's gravestone, Oisin slips from the stirrups and falls to the ground. Immediately he becomes an aged and feeble old man and can never return to Tir Na N-og.

The following are among the many themes students might discern in this story: Humans will always yearn for their earthly homes. It is impossible to escape aging and, finally, death. It is best to be satisfied with the happiness that you have.

In Celtic mythology, different pantheons of deities succeed each other over eons of time. The last of these groups was the Tuatha De Danaan, who were finally driven from power by human beings who were settling in Ireland. But these gods and goddesses did not die. Some, the *side*, went underground into the mounds of prehistoric Ireland. Others went to Tir fo Thuinn, The Land Under the Waves. Others went westward over the sea to Tir na N-og, the Land of Youth, where Time ceased to have meaning.

3. *Prometheus and Pandora* ◆ In this Greek myth, the god Prometheus enrages Zeus by bringing the gift of fire to human beings. With this gift, humans are able to make tremendous changes that improve their lives, which is exactly what Zeus did not want to happen. To punish Prometheus, Zeus tries to tempt him into marrying Pandora, a human woman created for this purpose and sent to earth carrying a mysterious lidded jar. The wary Prometheus gets his brother Epimetheus to marry Pandora instead. Epimetheus removes the lid from the jar, and a hoard of miseries escape to plague Earth forever. Still yearning for revenge, Zeus then has Prometheus chained to a mountaintop and sends an eagle to pluck at his body and eyes forever, or until Prometheus repents and swears allegiance to Zeus. Proud and stubborn, Prometheus endures his agony for thousands of years. Finally, Zeus relents and sends Hercules to break the chains and free the captive. One theme in the Prometheus segment of this story is that one must be ready to suffer to reach one's goals. A theme in the Pandora segment is that humans themselves bring about many of their own problems.

Early humans experienced fire only in its natural, rampaging, frightening form, as in forest fires or in flaming meteors that fell to earth. A culture hero like Prometheus, who brings fire to humans and teaches them how to control it, figures in the mythologies of most cultures and marks the beginning of civilized life; for fire, controlled, could be used for warmth, cooking, and smelting metals to make tools, weapons, and coins.

The Pandora segment of the story has many versions. In one of these versions, thought to have developed long after the one presented here, it is Pandora herself who opens the box and releases the pestilences. (If your students have read "Daughter of the Star" (pages 52-54), invite them to compare the story of Pandora with the story of Niachero.)

4. *Eldest Son and the Wrestling Match* ◆ In this Chippewa-Ojibwa myth, a young boy goes off on the traditional vision quest to find his adult name and his mission in life. Uppermost in his mind is his desire to find a way to provide a constant food source for his people. He is visited by his Guardian Spirit, who challenges him to a series of wrestling matches. Though the boy loses the first three matches, his courage and determination so impress the Great Sky Spirit and his Guardian Spirit that he is allowed to win the fourth match and ultimately gain his wish: from Guardian Spirit's body comes the first crop of corn. Dominant themes in this story are the importance of being courageous in the pursuit of one's goals and of choosing goals that benefit not just oneself, but all people.

Myths about the coming of corn abound in many Native American mythologies, because agriculture and husbandry released people from dependence on the vagaries of game animals and the wandering life followed perforce by hunters and

gatherers. This myth was recounted by Native American groups who lived on the shores of Lake Superior, in what are now the states of Minnesota and Wisconsin and the province of Ontario.

INTRODUCING THE SECTION

Have students look back at Activity Sheet 1 and read the sentences in the first column on the chart. Explain that (1) these sentences state the theme of the stories in Section 1; (2) a theme is the main idea in a story; (3) a theme or themes may not be stated directly in a story; it is up to the reader to put the different elements of a story together to come up with a good guess about the theme or themes. You might then write the following themes on the board and ask students to tell what stories in *Sections 2* and *3* develop the themes.

• Rulers must not forget their responsibilities to their people. "Plumed Serpent"

• Do not question the source of your good luck. "The Crane Wife"

• It takes great courage to establish peace in a land. "Theseus and the Minotaur"

Since good stories often have more than one theme, encourage students to state other themes they find in the stories above, and in other myths and legends they have read. Write students' ideas on the board. Discuss how themes in myths and legends state "words of wisdom" that often apply to all people, even today.

READING STRATEGY: THINK AS YOU READ

Distribute Activity Sheet 4 (page 107) and go over the directions with the class. Suggest that students work with a partner as they read the stories and complete the activity. Later, students can use the completed activity as they discuss the myths with the class.

See page 14 for additional reading strategies you may wish students to use in this unit.

QUESTIONS FOR DISCUSSION

1. Thor and His Hammer

• How does Thor lose his hammer? How does he get it back?

• In your opinion, was Thor justified in killing Frost Giants after he had his hammer back? Explain why or why not.

• What wisdom do you think Thor acquired as a result of this adventure? How might this wisdom be helpful to people today?

2. The Story of Oisin

• What positive human qualities does Oisin have? Give some examples of how he used these qualities.

• If you were in Oisin's place, would you have wanted to leave Tir Na N-og and visit Earth again? Explain why or why not.

• Oisin wants two things that conflict with one another. What are these things? Which of Oisin's needs is stronger? What lesson does he learn?

3. Prometheus and Pandora

• Why do you think Zeus wanted to keep fire exclusively for the gods and goddesses? Why did Prometheus disobey Zeus?

• According to the myth, why are humans afflicted with wars and other evils? In your opinion, which character in the myth is most responsible for bringing this about? Explain why you think so.

• Prometheus undergoes a terrible punishment for his disobedience. What's fantastic about the punishment? What real-life message about heroes or inventors does this punishment stand for?

4. Eldest Son and the Wrestling Match

• What does Eldest Son want to achieve in his Guardian Spirit Quest?

• In your opinion, what is the most difficult trial Eldest Son faces? Why is it so difficult?

• What kinds of quests do young people today go on? What do they hope to learn?

SUMMING UP

As a result of the class discussion, students may wish to change or add to their responses on Activity Sheet 4. Invite students to share their final "words of wisdom" and discuss how they might apply to people today.

FOLLOW-UP ACTIVITIES AND CURRICULAR LINKS

1. DRAMA ◆ Invite students to form cooperative groups and write and present a play adapting a myth in this section to modern times. Explain to the class that, as modern plays, these will have no gods or goddesses or fantastic events in them. Rather, groups will choose one of the thematic statements they've written on Activity Sheet 4 and develop a realistic play that has the same theme. You may wish to use some of the following questions to help students engender their own ideas:

• What if Thor were a modern detective who carelessly mislaid some vital evidence, which was then stolen by the very criminal he was trying to catch?

• What if Oisin were a world traveler who became a powerful leader in a distant land, then returned home to find that no one there knew him anymore?

• What if Prometheus were the inventor of a simple, inexpensive vehicle that did not pollute, who found himself laughed at and threatened by those who did not want people to have this vehicle?

• What if a young person discovered a new food source for the starving people of the world but had to keep the source secret for a whole year?

Groups can decide which theme they wish to dramatize, then reread the myth to find any events they can "modernize" and add other events and new characters. The group can also decide together on the general thrust of each scene, then appoint members to write a rough script for the group to consider and amend. Groups can appoint actors for the various roles and choose a narrator to link the scenes of the play. Other groups roles are: director, prop manager, scenery crew, sound effects and music crew, announcer.

Provide time for groups to practice their plays. Most groups will benefit from your attendance at one of their rehearsals. You can add to the success of their performance by giving suggestions about diction, volume, and body movement and facial expressions that help the actors portray the characters vividly.

2. VOCABULARY/ART ◆ The English names of four of the days of the week derive from the names of Norse gods. Some of your students may be interested in making and illustrating a weekly or monthly calendar which presents these four days, and the three others as well, with their original names. Students can illustrate each day-name. In the spaces below each name, students can either note a classroom activity that will happen on that day or make up a fanciful activity based on a legend or myth from this or another section. For students' reference, post a copy of the following chart.

DAY	ORIGIN OF NAME
Sunday	From Old English *sunnandaeg,* "day of the sun"
Monday	From Old English *monandaeg,* "day of the moon"
Tuesday	From *Tiw.* Tiw was the Norse god of war and the son of Odin, the chief Norse god.
Wednesday	From *Odin,* sometimes pronounced *"Woden."*
Thursday	From *Thor,* the Norse thunder god
Friday	From *Friya,* a Norse goddess and wife of Odin
Saturday	From *Saturn.* Saturn was a Roman God. He was a version of the ancient Greek god Cronus. Cronus was the father of Zeus.

3. SCIENCE ◆ Invite interested students to make a picture chart showing different sources of energy and examples of how this energy can be used. Students might begin by reviewing how humans used the heat energy of fire in "Prometheus and Pandora." Point out that energy is the capacity for doing work, such as changing the form or position of something. For example, fire can change the form of ore by melting it; a steam engine changes heat into mechanical energy to move something.

Students can also research (1) the use of energy from wind and water; (2) the use of solar energy; (3) the use of thermal energy, or heat from earth's core; (4) the use of nuclear energy; (5) the kinetic energy of their own muscles as they transfer it by moving objects. Students may wish to work with a partner to make models or give demonstrations to explain how the energy works in 1 and 5 above. You might conclude the activity by discussing examples of how the harnessing of energy has improved human life, as well as examples of how it has harmed our lives, as in the acid rain resulting from emissions from factory smokestacks. Students may wish to add a picture of Pandora's box to their display, listing within it the destructive results of some uses of energy.

4. SOCIAL STUDIES ◆ Invite students to research the different kinds of grains, such as wheat, rice, corn, barley, sorghum, oats, rye, and millet. Suggest that students use an outline map of the world and make a map legend to denote principal areas where the different types of grain are grown. Ask your researchers to find out at the same time how these different grains are used: for human consumption or for feeding livestock. For example, 50 percent of the U.S. corn crop today is used as cattle feed. Students many wish to discuss and debate how grain-growing areas can be most wisely used to solve the problem of hunger throughout the world.

5. ART ◆ Invite students to paint a frieze, or long decorative band to be displayed on a wall, showing some of the wonderful steeds that appear in old stories. They might begin with Suho's pony (see "How the Horse-Head Fiddle Came To Be," pages 33-35) and with the white horse that carried Oisin back to Ireland. (Since neither of these horses is named in the stories, students might wish to give them names.) Students can then do some research to find out about the winged horse Pegasus, who appears in many Greek myths; Raksh, the horse ridden by the mythic Persian hero Rustan; Sleipnir, the eight-legged horse of Odin; and the horses who pulled the chariot of Poseidon, the Greek god of the sea. When students complete the frieze, they might enjoy writing and reading to the class a brief narrative or descriptive poem that tells about each of the horses.

WISDOM

Name(s) _____

Wise Words

All good stories have themes in them. A theme is the main idea in a story. In myths and legends, the theme can be stated as a bit of wisdom or as a lesson that the characters have learned, and that you have learned, too, from reading the story.

As you finish each story, think about what the theme is in your opinion. A story may have more than one theme, so write a sentence for each theme you find. An example is given to get you started.

Story Title	Theme or Themes
THOR AND HIS HAMMER	Power can easily be taken away from you.
THE STORY OF OISIN	
PROMETHEUS AND PANDORA	
ELDEST SON AND THE WRESTLING MATCH	

To Think About: The themes you've written above should apply to people today. They should be Wise Words that you think all people should remember. Go over your theme statements to make sure they are as important now as they were in ages past.

THOR AND HIS HAMMER

SCANDINAVIA

High in the heavens above the northern lands lay Asgard, the home of the gods and goddesses. Odin was their ruler, but their chief protector was Thor, the thunder god. With his magic hammer, Thor guarded Asgard from the Frost Giants, who were always seeking ways to invade Odin's kingdom. Thor's job required constant vigilance. He rode about the skies in his chariot, keeping track of the Frost Giants' whereabouts. Often, Loki the trickster god accompanied Thor on this endless patrol.

The deities of those days slept and ate as ordinary humans do. One night, as Thor and Loki slumbered by the side of a brook, one of the Frost Giants stole Thor's hammer and carried it to the Frost King. When Thor and Loki awoke and saw that the hammer was missing, they were filled with alarm.

"How shall I defend Asgard now?" cried Thor. "Surely the Frost Giants will come to Asgard and take our stronghold!"

"We must get the hammer back," said Loki, "and I think I know the way to do this. Let us go to the goddess Freyja and borrow her falcon garment."

Now, Freyja was the goddess of love and beauty, and since love and beauty have many forms, Freyja often went about in disguises. The falcon garment, made of strong and shining feathers, was one of these, and whoever put it on looked just like a bird.

In Thor's chariot, the thunder god and Loki rode to Freyja's palace. "Asgard is in great danger," Thor said to the goddess, "for the Frost Giants now have my hammer, and without it I am helpless to protect our kingdom. Pray lend us your falcon garment, Freyja."

"I shall put it on and fly to the land of the Frost Giants," said Loki. "I shall try to trick them into giving the hammer back."

"For this great purpose," answered Freyja, "I would lend you my garment even if it were made of gold and silver."

So, donning the winged garment, Loki flew to Utgard, the icy caves of the Frost Giants, where he found their king making golden collars for his dogs and silver bridles for his horses. The king was not fooled by Loki's disguise. "Ah, Loki," he said, "how goes it in Asgard?"

"As if you did not know!" said Loki. "I am here to fetch the hammer of Thor, which one of your people has stolen from us."

"And do you think I would be so foolish as to return the hammer," laughed the Frost King, "after I have gone to all this trouble to get it? I have buried the hammer deep in the ice, where you will never find it. There is only one from Asgard to whom I will give the hammer, and that is the goddess Freyja, if she will come to me and be my wife!"

Now, Loki did not know what to say to this. He turned and flew away from Utgard and went back to Thor and Freyja, who were waiting anxiously outside her palace. "Did you bring it?" asked Thor. "Did you get my hammer?"

Loki explained the bargain the Frost King wished to make. Then bowing to Freyja, Loki said, "It is up to you to marry the Frost King, my lady. Otherwise, all Asgard is doomed."

"Marry the Frost King!" sputtered Freyja. "That I will never do! I will never leave Asgard to marry that cruel, hideous giant and live in his ice-covered, bitter cold kingdom."

"But then what should we do?" pleaded Thor.

"I do not know," said Freyja, turning away from him. "It is your fault the hammer is gone, and thus it is your responsibility to get it back." And sternly she left him and went into her palace.

Swiftly Thor and Loki went to the court of Odin and told him what had happened to the hammer and how

Freyja had refused to marry the Frost King.

"This calls for a council of all the gods and goddeses of Asgard," said Odin. He summoned them to him, and for hours the deities pondered the situation without coming up with a solution.

At last Heimdall, who was the watchman of the rainbow, said, "Let us dress Thor in Freyja's garments, braid his long golden hair, and give him a bridal veil. Disguised in this way, he can go to Utgard as the Frost King's bride. Once the wedding ceremony is over, the Frost King will give his bride the hammer, as he promised he would do."

Thor protested, but Loki said, "Listen, this is a good plan of Heimdall's. And you need not go to Utgard alone. I will dress as your bridesmaid and attend you."

And so the gods and goddesses of Asgard braided Thor's golden hair and dressed him as a bride, with a long, heavy veil to cover his face. And Loki was true to his promise and decked himself out as the bride's attendant. Clothed in this way, the two gods descended to Utgard.

The Frost King was overjoyed to think he had actually won the fair Freyja as a wife. He ordered a huge wedding feast to be prepared and called all his subjects to attend. But the King looked astounded as he watched his bride eat, lifting huge portions of food to her mouth under her heavy veil. For Thor was always a good eater, and this time he ate a whole ox, eight salmon, and three casks of mead.

"Never have I seen a woman eat so much!" exclaimed the King.

But Loki whispered into the King's ear, "Freyja has been so excited and happy about this wedding that she has not been able to eat for eight days, your majesty."

This answer pleased the Frost King. "Come," he said, "Let me lift your veil, my bride, so that I may give you a kiss."

But when the King lifted the veil, such beams of light shot from Thor's eyes that the King stepped back in alarm. "Why does my bride have such sharp eyes?" he exclaimed.

Again Loki whispered to him. "Her eyes shine from fatigue," he said, "for she has been unable to sleep for eight nights, so excited and happy she has been as she thought of her wedding."

This answer, too, pleased the Frost King. "Let the hammer be brought forth as my gift to my bride!" he commanded. As the king's servants left to retrieve the hammer from its icy grave, Thor could scarcely maintain his composure. And when the hammer was finally laid in his lap, he took it in his hands, threw off his disguise and stood in all his mighty splendor as the thunder god.

Wielding his mighty hammer, Thor swept down upon the Frost Giants and killed many of them. Then he and Loki returned triumphant to Asgard, which now once again was saved. Thor was careful to never again let his hammer leave his fist. And his strength became even greater, for Odin gave him a magic belt, which doubled his power when he tightened it, and an iron glove to use when he threw thunderbolts. ♦

THE STORY OF OISIN

IRELAND

here was a mystic land called Tir Na N-og, or the Land of the Blessed. It was in the clouds and beyond the Western Sea, and no one ever grew old there. The King of Tir Na N-og had ruled there forever, and yet he was afraid that someone might take his throne from him.

The king called his Druid, or wiseman, to him and asked, "Will I always rule in Tir Na N-og?"

"That you shall," said the Druid. "Unless your daughter marries. Then her husband will rule in your place."

Now, the Princess was a kind and beautiful woman, and the king loved her. But he did not love her as much as he loved his own power. So he called his daughter to him and said, "I shall make sure that no man ever wants to marry you!" And with that, the king changed the girl's head into the head of a pig.

The girl wept bitterly, and the Druid was filled with remorse that he had given such information to the king.

"Listen to me, my dear," said the Druid. "You need not have this pig's head forever. If you go back to Erin and find Oisin, the son of Finn MacCumhail, and if you can convince him to marry you, then your own lovely face will be restored. Furthermore, you will have for yourself one of the finest young men on Earth as a husband, for Oisin is as wise and kind as he is brave and strong. Bring him back here to Tir Na N-og, and he shall be King."

The Princess stopped her weeping just a bit. She said, "And how am I going to convince a man to marry a woman with a pig's head?"

"Ah, that I truly do not know," said the Druid, scratching his head. "You will have to use your ingenuity."

The Princess was filled with doubt, but there seemed no other path to take. Descending through the clouds from Tir Na N-og to Erin, she found herself in a thick forest. The sound of axes felling trees sounded not far away, and all about her feet lay piles of cut wood. Soon the sound of chopping stopped, and the Princess heard the laughter of young men coming closer and closer. Quickly she hid behind a tree.

Four handsome lads appeared. "Now that we've got a good supply of firewood here," said one of them, "we must carry it back to our father's home."

"Not I!" said another lad. "I am too tired."

"We'll cut wood but not carry it!" said the other two.

"Then who is to do it, brothers?" asked the first young man.

"Do it youself, Oisin," the three laughed. And they left him and went away.

Oisin sat down, quite discouraged. "I can't carry all this wood!" he muttered to himself.

The Princess, trembling with fear but determined to conquer it, stepped out from behind the tree. "Perhaps I can help you," she said shyly to Oisin.

Oisin leapt to his feet, thoroughly startled. "Upon my word!" he exclaimed. "Never have I seen such an ugly woman!"

"I was not always thus," said the Princess, begining to weep again. "My face was once as fair as any woman's in Erin. Will you listen to my story?"

"Most willingly," said Oisin, sitting down again.

And so the Princess told him of the cruel enchantment, and of how she would regain her own face only if he, Oisin, would consent to marry her, and of how Oisin would then become King of Tir Na N-og.

"If that's the situation," said Oisin, "why, I'll marry you immediately!"

And he did, and immediately the Princess's pig head was replaced with her own beautiful one.

"Now, my dear husband," said the princess, "I cannot stay here in Erin any longer. Come, follow me back to the Land of the Blessed." She took Oisin's hand and led him through clouds and mist to Tir Na N-og.

In that mystical place, the old King welcomed his daughter, for he was deeply sorry for what he had done to her. Gladly he handed over his throne to his new son-in-law. Now Oisin was King, and his bride was the Queen of this land of youth and beauty.

The time passed swiftly because it was a time of happy days. In Tir Na N-og, there was always feasting and games and music and laughter. Oisin felt blessed indeed to be ruler of such a pleasant kingdom. But after a while, he began to think about his father and his brothers and his friends and his home in Erin. He was curious to see how they were faring and sad to think that he might never see his aging father again. Oisin shared these thoughts with his wife.

"Ah, dear husband," said the Queen. "How long do you think you have been here?"

"About three years," said Oisin.

"No, you have been here for three *hundred* years," said his wife. "All the people you long to see in Erin have long since died. Even the land itself is different. You would recognize very little there. Be content here. Stay with me."

But Oisin grew insistent. "Just once," he said. "I want to go back to Erin just once. Then I shall return to you."

"There is only one way you can do that," said the Queen. "You must ride my white horse through the mist to your homeland. But you must never get off the horse. If your foot so much as touches the ground, you will be lost to me forever."

"Then my foot shall never touch the ground," promised Oisin. "Have the white horse brought to me."

The horse was a marvel of strength and beauty, with soft, intelligent eyes, and swift as the wind. Mounting this steed, Oisin bade farewell to the Queen, assuring her again that he would return quickly. The Queen watched as the horse galloped into the clouds, bearing her beloved husband. Then she turned away.

In no time at all, Oisin was in Erin. He rode through the countryside toward his father's home. How strange the land looked. The forests were almost gone. "My brothers have been busy at their woodcutting, I see!" thought Oisin. Stranger still, nearing his father's land, he saw no barns or cottages, only heaps of stone.

And when he reached the place where his father's house had stood, there was only a mass of rocks and weeds.

Oisin began to weep. "It is as my wife told me," he cried. Everything I once knew is now gone! I shall return to Tir Na N-og."

As he turned the reins to head back, he spied an old man coming along the road.

"I say there, my good man," called Oisin. "What has become of the great family of Finn MacCumhail, the family that once dwelled here? Are there none of them left?"

The old man looked at him quizzically. "Ah, sir," he said. "They all died long, long ago. Long before I was born. Indeed, long before my grandmother was born! See," he said, kicking away with his boot a tuft of grass. "There is the old, mouldering tombstone of Finn MacCumhail himself."

"Please hand it up to me," said Oisin. "I wish to read what it says."

"Get down from your horse and do it yourself!" said the old man. "I am an old, weak fellow, and you are young and strong!" And with that the old man went on his way.

Oisin leaned from his saddle, reaching down for the tombstone. Farther and farther over he leaned, as the horse whinnied in alarm.

Just as his hand was almost touching the tip of the stone, Oisin's foot slipped from the stirrup, his toe touched the ground, and he fell from the saddle. The great white horse bolted away and stood mournfully at a distance, staring at the man who had been his rider. Just a moment ago so strong and young, Oisin was now withered and ancient.

"Come, White Horse," said Oisin, his voice crackled with age. "Carry me back to Tir Na N-og!"

But this of course, could not be done. The horse bowed its head in farewell, and then disappeared into the mists, returning to the Land of the Blessed where the Queen stood sadly waiting. ◆

PROMETHEUS AND PANDORA

GREECE

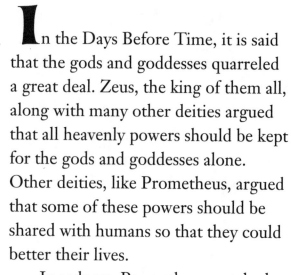

In the Days Before Time, it is said
that the gods and goddesses quarreled
a great deal. Zeus, the king of them all,
along with many other deities argued
that all heavenly powers should be kept
for the gods and goddesses alone.
Other deities, like Prometheus, argued
that some of these powers should be
shared with humans so that they could
better their lives.

In sadness, Prometheus watched
men and women crawling about
the Earth, with no way to keep warm
in winter's blast, no way to make
tools. "It is fire they need," thought
Prometheus, "fire, until now the pos-
session of Zeus alone. But I shall bring
fire from the heavens to Earth, though
Zeus forbids it."

To carry out his plan, Prometheus
had to be stealthy. With a single
branch of wood, he lit a fire from the

flaming wheels of the chariot that carried the sun across the skies. Prometheus carried this flaming torch to Earth and thus delivered fire to humans.

With Prometheus's gift, human life underwent a remarkable change. Now humans could cook their food or smoke and preserve it for later use. With the warmth of fire, people could survive the bitterest winters. With the heat of fire, humans could smelt metals and turn them into tools to use for agriculture. With fire, people could also form metals into art objects and make coins to use in commerce with distant groups of humans. All human life became better as a result of Prometheus's daring deed.

But Zeus was furious at what Prometheus had done and racked his mind for a way to punish this upstart and return humans to a life of hardship.

Finally, Zeus hit upon a solution. In concert with the other gods and goddesses, he made a woman who was exemplary in every way, and he named her Pandora. She was designed to appeal to Prometheus, for she had beauty, wisdom, and wit. Zeus gave this lovely woman an exquisite lidded jar and sent her to Earth.

"Prometheus," announced Zeus, "Pandora is the perfect wife for you, for she has all the qualities you admire."

Now, Prometheus was too wise not to suspect a gift from Zeus, and so he suggested to his brother Epimetheus that he marry Pandora instead. Epimetheus was more than willing, and he and Pandora were wed.

"But what is it that you carry in that lidded jar?" asked Epimetheus of his bride.

"I don't know," said Pandora. "I know only that Zeus told me never to open it."

What more could one say to arouse curiosity? One night, when Pandora was sleeping, Epimetheus quietly removed the jar's lid. Immediately the room, and all the World, was filled with a furious buzzing and humming and stinging. Dreadful things were released from the jar: war and sickness and despair and anger; suspicion and hunger and feuds and doubt. These torments went flying over the world of humans, changing their peaceful life into discord.

But unbeknownst to Zeus, Athena had put something into the jar that could help to allay all these

the end of time," thundered Zeus. "And to add to your miseries, I shall send my eagle to pluck away at your eyes and your body for eternity. You will never be released until you beg my forgiveness and swear to me your eternal allegiance and obedience."

Prometheus laughed bitterly. "That I shall never do, Mighty Zeus," he said defiantly. And so he remained chained and tortured for many centuries, some say for thirty thousand years. But never in all this time was Prometheus forgotten by humans. Indeed, he was honored by them for the gift of fire, and many gifts and prayers were offered to him.

In time, Zeus, worried that Prometheus was so loved by humans, and understanding that he would never relent, decided to free him. But who could break the unbreakable chains? There was only one being strong enough, and that was Hercules. And so it was this mighty giant who broke Prometheus's bonds and slew the eagle who had caused him such agony. The young god strode down from the mountaintop, as strong and defiant as he had ever been and went about the world of humans to find still more ways to help them. ◆

miseries, and this thing was Hope. And Hope flew out all over the world to serve as a balance to the woes that had escaped from Pandora's jar.

Zeus's anger at Prometheus was not allayed. After all, this young god had not only dared to argue with him but had also defied him and stolen fire from him. He had given a gift to humans that Zeus never intended them to have.

To punish Prometheus for his rebellion, Zeus hit upon a terrible revenge. He ordered some of the minor gods to capture Prometheus and chain him with unbreakable links to the top of Mount Caucauses. "There among the rocks and wind you shall stay until

ELDEST SON AND THE WRESTLING MATCH

•••••••••••••••••••••••••

NORTH AMERICA
CHIPPEWA-OJIBWA

In the time before people counted time, there was a good man who had several children. The father had difficulty feeding them all, for this was in the days when people only got food by hunting animals or gathering berries and nuts. Game was not always plentiful, and the land was not always fruitful. Eldest Son grieved when his young brothers and sisters had to go hungry.

Now, one spring Eldest Son reached the age when he was to go away to pursue his Guardian Spirit Quest. All young boys looked forward to this time, for the boy would find his special name and discover the special power that would be given to him by his Guardian Spirit. The Quest was never easy. The boy had to go off into an isolated place, build a shelter, and go without food for seven days.

Eldest Son went on his Quest with a serious, happy heart. He walked through the forest for two days, observing everything around him with great respect, and thinking to himself, "I wish I could find a way for my people to get enough food without hunting animals every day to eat."

On the third day, weak with hunger, Eldest Son built himself a shelter and lay down to rest. "Perhaps in my dreams," he thought, "I will come upon a way to help my people."

And in his dream, it happened that way. Eldest Son saw a man coming down from the sky, dressed in green and yellow colors and wearing a plume of waving feathers on his head.

"I am your Guardian Spirit," said the sky-visitor. "I have been sent to you by the Sky Chief. The Sky Chief knows the kind and worthy wish in your secret heart and is pleased that you do not seek to use your strength to make war. He has given you the spirit name Wunzh. And I am sent to test you and to show you how to obtain your wish."

Then the sky-visitor ordered Wunzh to wrestle with him. This was a great challenge for a boy weak from lack of food. But Wunzh did as he was told and wrestled with his Guardian Spirit. Just as the boy was about to give up in exhaustion, the sky-visitor stopped and rose.

"This is enough for today," he said. "I shall come back tomorrow to test you again."

The next day at the same time Wunzh's Guardian Spirit appeared, and the wrestling match began again. Wunzh felt his courage increasing, and he put all his mind and heart into the task. Still, he could feel himself weakening. But just before he fell to the ground, the Guardian Spirit stopped the match.

"Tomorrow will be your last chance," said the spirit. "I urge you to be strong, for this is the only way you will achieve your secret wish."

Wunzh dropped exhausted to his bed. He had only enough strength left to pray to the Sky Chief for the courage to endure the next wrestling match. And when the Guardian Spirit reappeared the next day, the boy drove forward with endurance and determination. Though his legs felt like rubber and his arms were weak, Wunzh wrestled on. Again the Guardian Spirit stopped the match. But this time he declared himself conquered by Wunzh.

"Listen to me, Wunzh," said the spirit. "Because you have wrestled manfully and courageously, the Great Sky Chief has granted your secret desire. Now listen well to my final instructions to you. Tomorrow is your seventh day of fasting. We will wrestle again, and you will prevail over me. When I fall to the ground, clean the earth of roots and weeds and make the ground soft. Then bury me in the very spot where I have fallen and cover the spot with my yellow and green clothes and then with soil.

"When you have done this, leave my body in the earth and do not disturb it. Come back once a month to see that no weeds or grass cover my grave. Cover me with fresh soil. If you follow my instructions, you will succeed in your Guardian Spirit Quest. You will help your family and all your people by teaching them what I have taught you."

When the Guardian Spirit returned the next day, Wunzh felt himself filled with superhuman strength and easily threw his opponent to the ground. He then followed in every detail the burial instructions his Guardian had given him and finally returned weary and exhausted and starving to his parents' lodge.

All that spring and summer, Wunzh returned faithfully to the grave of his Guardian Spirit, tending and cleaning it and keeping the ground soft and pliable as he had been instructed. In midsummer, the boy noticed the tops of green plumes emerging through the earth. He noticed, too, that the more care he gave the plants the faster the plumes grew. By summer's end, the plumes were topped with silken hair,

and gold clusters clung to each side of each stalk. It was only then that Wunzh understood how his Quest had been rewarded and how his secret wish had been granted. It was only then that Wunzh felt free to bring his father to this secret place where his Guardian Spirit lay buried.

"Father," said Wunzh, "these are the plants from my Guardian Spirit, whose name is Mon daw-min, or 'corn for all people.' This is the answer to my Quest! No longer will we have to depend solely on animals and berries for our food! As long as we care for the earth, the earth will give us this food!"

Then Wunzh showed his father how the husks should be pulled from the stalks and how some of the seeds must be saved for planting for the next season. He showed how to hold the corn in the fire just long enough for the outer leaves to turn brown, while the kernels remained sweet and juicy.

Wunzh's family and his people held a Feast of Corn and thanked the Great Sky Spirit for this gift. As for Wunzh, he thanked his Guardian Spirit, too, and was grateful that his wish had been granted and that his Spirit Quest had been successfully completed. ◆

PRONUNCIATION GUIDE

Aegean Sea (ih JEE uhn) _____

Aegeus (EE jee us) _____

Aethra (EE thrah) _____

Asgard (AZ gard) _____

Arachne (uh RACK nee) _____

Ariadne (air ee ADD nee) _____

Artemis (ART uh mis) _____

Athena (uh THEE nuh) _____

Athens (A thins) _____

Atlas (AT lus) _____

August Personage (aw GUST   PUR sun ij)

_____

Bahman (BAH mun) _____

Boeotia (bee OH shuh) _____

Chih-nii (SHEE NEE) _____

Chios (KEE us) _____

Crete (KREET) _____

Daedalus (DED uh lus) _____

Demeter (DEM uh ter) _____

Druid (DROO id) _____

Epimetheus (ep uh ME thee us) _____

_____

Erin (ERR uhn) _____

Finn MacCumhail (FIN   mik COM uhl) _____

_____

Freyja (FRAY uh) _____

Hades (HAY dees) _____

Hah-yah-no (hah YAH no) _____

Haumea (hah oo MAY uh) _____

Heimdall (IM doll) _____

Helios (HEE lee us) _____

Hercules (HUR kyu leez) _____

Hermes (HUR meez) _____

Hi ' iaka (HI ee AH kah) _____

Hyrieus (HUR ee us) _____

Kauai (KOO ay) _____

Khan (KAHN) _____

Labyrinth (LAB uh rinth) _____

Lohiau (lo ee AH oo) _____

Loki (LO kee) _____

Maui (MOW ee) _____

Mblukwa (um BLOOK wah) _____

Merope (MAYR ope ee) _____

Minos (MY nos) _____

Minotaur (MIN uh tor) _____

Moemoe (MO eh MO eh) _____

Moku-a-weoweo (MO koo ah WAY oh WAY oh)

_____

Mo'o (MO O) _____

Mount Caucauses (KO kuh sus) _____

_____

Niachero (NEE ah CHER oh) _____

_____

Nymphs (NIMFS) _____

Oahu (o AH hoo) _____

Odin (O din) _____

Oisin (o SHEEN) _____

Olepau (o lay PAH oo) _____

Olympus (o LIM puhs) _____

Orion (o RY un) _____

Pandora (pan DOR uh) _____

Parizade (par ee ZAHD) _____

Pele (PAY LAY) _____

Persephone (per SEF uh nee) _____

Perviz (pur VEEZ) _____

Pleiades (PLAY uh deez) _____

Pleione (PLAY ee ohn) _____

Poseidon (po SY dun) _____

Procrustes (pro CRUST eez) _____

Prometheus (pro ME thee us) _____

Pwalo (PWA lo) _____

Quetzalcoatl (ket SAL koh AHT ul) _____

_____

Sciron (SY ron) _____

Sinis (SI nus) _____

Sirius (SYR ee us) _____

Suho (SOO HO) _____

Sultaness (sul TAHN us) _____

Sultan Khos'roo Shah (SUL tahn KOS roo SHA)

_____

Tezcatlipoca (Tezz CAT li Pocah) _____

Theseus (THEE see us) _____

Thor (THOR) _____

Tir Na N-og (teer nah NOHG) _____

_____

Toltecs (TOHL teks) _____

Tula (TOO luh) _____

Utgard (OOT gard) _____

Wunzh (WUN zeh) _____

Zeus (ZOOZ) _____

BIBLIOGRAPHY

The books recommended below are excellent for reading aloud or for independent reading. Many of them are picture books, suitable for readers of all ages, whose illustrations not only add to the drama of the story but also give visual insights into the cultures of the people who tell these legends and myths.

COLLECTIONS

Belting, Natalie. *The Earth Is on a Fish's Back*. Holt, 1965. (Twenty-one origin myths and legends from around the world)

DeSpain, Pleasant. *Thirty-Three Multicultural Tales To Tell*. August, 1993.

Hamilton, Virginia. *In the Beginning: Creation Stories from Around the World*. Harcourt, 1988.

Mayo, Margaret. *Magical Tales from Many Lands*. Dutton, 1993.

Passes, David. *Dragons: Truth, Myth, and Legend*. Western/Arists & Writers Guild, 1993.

THE MIDDLE EAST

Al-Saleh, Khairat. *Fabled Cities, Princes & Jinn from Arab Myths and Legends*. Schocken, 1985.

Mayer, Maranna. *Alladin and the Enchanted Lamp*. Macmillan, 1985.

Stories from the Arabian Nights. Retold by Naomi Lewis. Holt, 1987.

Zeman, Ludmilla. *The Revenge of Ishtar*. Tundra, 1993. (The Gilgamesh myth from ancient Mesopotamia)

EUROPE

de Gerez, Toni. *Louhi, Witch of North Farm: A Finnish Tale*. Viking, 1986. (Retelling of part of the Kalevala, Finland's great epic)

dePaola, Tomie. *Prince of the Dolomites*. Harcourt, 1980. (An Italian moon legend)

Evslin, Bernard. *The Minotaur*. Chelsea House, 1987.

Fisher, Leonard Everett. *The Olympians: Great Gods and Goddesses of Ancient Greece*. Holiday, 1984.

Fonteyn, Margot. *Swan Lake*. Harcourt, 1989. (The Russian legend on which the ballet is based)

Hodges, Margaret. *Saint George and the Dragon: A Golden Legend*. Little, Brown, 1984. (A retelling of Edmund Spenser's sixteenth century legend)

Hutton, Warwick. *Perseus*. Macmillan/Margaret K. McElderry, 1993.

Hutton, Warwick. *Theseus and the Minotaur*. Macmillan/Margaret K. McElderry, 1990.

McCaughrean, Geraldine. *Greek Myths*. Macmillan/Margaret K. McElderry, 1993.

McDermott, Beverly Brodsky. *The Golem: A Jewish Legend*. Lippincott, 1976. (From Czechoslovakia)

Price, Margaret Evans. *Myths and Enchantment Tales.* Rand, 1960. (Greek heroines and heroes, with their Roman names)

San Souci, Robert D. *Young Merlin.* Doubleday, 1990 (Introduction to the Arthurian legends)

Sutcliff, Rosemary. *Black Ships Before Troy: The Story of the Iliad.* Delacorte, 1993.

Turska, Krystyna. *The Magician of Cracow.* Greenwillow, 1975. (A Polish moon legend)

Yolen, Jane. *The Greyling.* Philomel, 1991. (Selchi legends from Scotland about seals that take on human forms)

Zvorykin, Boris, & Onassis, J. *The Firebird.* Viking, 1978. (The Russian legend of Prince Ivan)

THE AMERICAS

Belting, Natalia M. *Moon Was Tired of Walking.* Houghton, 1992. (Fourteen origin myths from ten different South American tribes)

Blanco, Alberto. *The Desert Mermaid/La Sirena del Desierto.* Children's Book Press, 1992. (A legend from Mexico)

Bruhac, Joseph. *Flying with the Eagle, Racing the Great Bear: Stories from Native North America.* Bridgewater, 1993.

Ehlert, Lois. *Moon Rope/Un Lazo a la Luna.* Harcourt, 1992. (Peruvian legend in English and Spanish)

Ginsburg, Mirra. *The Proud Maiden, Tungak, and the Sun.* Macmillan, 1974. (An Eskimo legend)

Goble, Paul. *Star Boy.* Bradbury, 1983. (A myth of the Blackfeet)

Harris, Christie. *Mouse Woman and the Mischief Makers.* Atheneum, 1977. (Legends of Canadian Indians of the Northwest coast)

Hamilton, Virginia. *The People Could Fly.* Knopf, 1985. (African-American legends and folktales)

Haviland, Virginia. *North American Legends.* Putnam, 1979. (Legends of African-Americans, Native Americans, and European Americans)

Martin, Eva. *Tales of the Far North.* Dial, 1987. (Canadian legends)

Martinez, Alejandro Cruz. *The Woman Who Outshone the Sun.* Children's Book Press, 1991. (Zapotec legend in English and Spanish)

Melzcak, Ronald. *Raven, Creator of the World.* Little, Brown, 1970. (Eskimo origin myths)

Robinson, Gail. *Raven the Trickster: Legends of North American Indians.* Atheneum, 1982.

Taylor, C. J. *How We Saw the World: Nine Native Stories of the Way Things Began.* Tundra, 1993.

Taylor, C. J. *The Secret of the White Buffalo: An Ogala Legend.* Tundra, 1993.

ASIA

Birdseye, Tom. *A Song of Stars.* Holiday, 1990. (Chinese myth of the stars Vega and Altair)

Chatterjee, Debjani. *The Elephant-Headed God and other Hindu Tales.* Oxford, 1992.

Dalal-Clayton, Diksha. *The Adventures of Young Krishna: The Blue God of India.* Oxford, 1992.